CULTIVATING ATTENTION

The Paradoxical Secret
of Team Success

JOSEPH H. ANDERSON

KERYKEION PRESS
Seattle, Washington

Kerykeion Press, Seattle
© 2019 Joseph H. Anderson Consulting, LLC
www.jhanderson.biz

ISBN: 978-1-7335234-0-0

Book design by Victoria Scarlett

The words of truth are always paradoxical.

To the mind that is still,

the whole universe surrenders.

- Laozi

For Victoria

CONTENTS

INTRODUCTION
The paradox of effective teams

A paradox is a seemingly absurd statement
that turns out to be true.

Leaders, organizations and teams often behave as though
working harder and thinking harder will ensure the results they
want. It seems absurd that anything else would lead to higher
team productivity. And yet there's ample evidence that working
harder and thinking harder isn't enough.

Consider these retrospective meeting comments:

- "We worked hard, but we got distracted and failed to focus on what was truly important."
- "We put in a ton of effort but couldn't overcome the factions and trust issues on the team."
- "We thought hard, but we got caught in assumptions that turned out to be wrong."
- "We put in long hours but spent all our time rushing from one crisis to the next in a panic."

The paradox is that a team's success comes from its ability to work and think *together*, not work and think *harder*.

There are plenty of clues that this is so. "Psychological safety" is the number one reason teams at Google are effective. [1] "Healthy culture" is the key factor driving success in DevOps[2] and Agile[3] transformations, CRM implementations[4], and digital transformations[5]. "Lack of emotional maturity" is one of the top reasons large-scale technology initiatives fail. [6]

Unfortunately, there is no product that reliably installs psychological safety, healthy culture, and emotional maturity in teams. Instead, organizations typically do one of two things: they ignore these human qualities entirely, or they pay lip service in one way or another (maybe a cursory presentation or two, maybe an employee wellness program). But most organizations still end up trying to improve results the old-fashioned way, by pushing their teams to work and think harder. Is it any wonder that in a recent survey nearly 60% of tech workers reported feeling burned out?[7]

This book offers a simple prescription for teams to get results. Its paradoxical premise is that teams can most rapidly and reliably improve their effectiveness by cultivating just one skill: paying attention. As a happy by-product, this skill, when applied to relationships, thinking, and emotions, also creates the psychological safety, healthy culture, and emotional maturity that the research points to as essential for team success. The main benefit, though, is that by paying attention teams deliver results.

What it takes for teams to succeed

I've been working on technology teams for nearly thirty years. I started as a technical writer and grew from there into a team manager. For the last ten years or so I've been a product and program manager, where my most important job has been helping cross-functional teams collaborate more effectively. I have worked with teams at software companies large and small, non-profits, and consulting firms. I've led teams and been a key individual contributor. I've coordinated large cross-functional teams, managed matrixed teams, assembled and led ad hoc teams of contractors, started local offices, and launched new teams inside existing organizations. A lot of those projects were successful, and some weren't. A few of those projects were among the best, most exhilarating human experiences I've ever had—and a few were among the worst. And in that regard, I'm the same as every other leader and team member I know.

Any leader or team member can point to an initiative they are proud of, that went off smoothly and left them smiling. What are those teams like? They have a shared understanding of their work, the context of that work, and each other. They are able to act together to achieve a common goal. They understand the larger context of the work, including their organization's mission, its partners, and the populations it serves. They understand the individuals, teams and partners they collaborate with.

In short, a successful team is **aligned**.

An aligned team delivers expected results on time. They make customers and stakeholders happy, and by fulfilling their purpose they are happy themselves.

Consider the actions of a team that meets the above definition:

- They focus on the right priorities. They concentrate on the goal they're trying to accomplish, make adjustments as needed, and get across the finish line. Out of the swirl of things that could be done, they avoid distraction and consistently work on the things that should be done. In other words, they have the habit of Stable Attention.
- They collaborate well together. They make relationships a top priority and actively listen and pay attention to each other. Changes of team personnel or leadership aren't disruptive, because new members are incorporated with relative ease. In other words, they have the habit of Connectedness.
- They make great decisions that stick and really work, because they think things through. Rather than jumping to

conclusions, they challenge their assumptions, and can see and evaluate the facts as they are. When differences of opinion arise, they don't take it personally but engage in open and lively debate. In other words, they have the habit of Open-Mindedness.

- They show resilience in the face of adversity. When threats appear, they pay attention to their experience and work through any reactions together rather than being swept away by them. The team is an emotionally safe place where tough times can be weathered gracefully. In other words, they have the habit of **Self-Awareness**.

Why team alignment is hard

Happy accidents may result in teams staying aligned. Through a combination of leadership, circumstances, personalities, and luck, a team may stumble into a rhythm of alignment that carries them to success. But this combination of winning qualities is frustratingly difficult to preserve or reproduce. For many teams in many organizations much of the time, alignment is a struggle, and the wins don't happen often enough. And given our increasingly complex, diverse, and geographically distributed work environments, it's getting less and less likely the wins will happen by chance. Why is it so hard for teams to stay aligned?

The unfortunate truth is that the habits that lead to alignment—stable attention, connectedness, open-mindedness, and self-awareness—don't come naturally. They are countered by neurological capabilities our ancestors developed millennia ago.

These capabilities equipped humans for survival in our ancestral landscape. Without them, we wouldn't be here today as a species. It's not too strong to call them **survival optimizations**. We should be grateful for them…and yet they can get in our way and create complications. Consider these characteristics of your brain:

- Your brain is **busy**. Your cognitive circuits are optimized to think all the time, constantly evaluating and theorizing about the opportunities and threats in your environment, as well as ruminating on memories about the past and developing predictions of the future. This constant thinking enables you to solve problems, avoid danger, and explore new possibilities. But this very same survival optimization means you can easily become so distracted and lost in thought that you don't even notice what's going on.

- Your brain is **tribal**. Your brain constantly evaluates other people as possible threats or possible allies, skewing your experience of other humans to prioritize self-protection and protection of your group. This attention to social relationships enables you to build community, find safety in numbers, and act together with your tribe to make amazing things happen. But this very same survival optimization means you can just as rapidly construct tribal boundaries that kill the potential for collaboration.

- Your brain is **biased**. For survival purposes, your decision-making apparatus is optimized to decide quickly and efficiently, making snap judgments about what's really going on without wasting time to question your assumptions. The ability to think quickly enables you to take action against a threat in a heartbeat, solve simple problems with dazzling speed, and come up with inventive solutions on the spot. But this very same survival optimization means that you can make terrible decisions based on bad assumptions without ever stopping to notice.

- Your brain is **reactive**. Both your brain and your body are optimized to act immediately to perceived threats, orchestrating physiological and cognitive reactions to fight, or run away, or hide. The ability to react instinctively enables you to avoid immediate physical danger with great efficiency. But this very same survival optimization also means you're reacting all the time—even when you're not in danger—and sending your body and your mind in entirely unproductive directions.

The impact of the survival optimizations

Remember those project-destroying, budget-consuming, staff-wasting and customer-infuriating retrospective outcomes I mentioned earlier? A substantial part of the blame for them goes to the survival optimizations. If your team said:

- "We got distracted and didn't focus on what was truly important"—that's a sign the busy brain has been at work, compromising your ability to maintain stable attention.
- "We had trust issues"—that's because the tribal brain has been doing its thing, breaking down the interpersonal connectedness you need to be successful.

- "We made assumptions that turned out to be wrong"—you can be sure that the biased brain has played a role in weakening your ability to stay open-minded.
- "We spent all our time rushing from one crisis to the next in a panic"—it's likely that the reactive brain has been consuming your attention and inhibiting your self-awareness.

Project failures happen because team members' brains are functioning as they were built to function. And yet, if any team is going to build the habits of alignment so projects can succeed, they will have to do something about the survival optimizations.

Paying attention: the key to aligning your team

"If these survival optimizations are so fundamental to the functioning of the brain," you might ask, "isn't it impossible to do anything about them?" It does take work to change these built-in behaviors and acquire new habits—but it can be done. There is really **just one change you need to make** to counter the effects of the ancient survival optimizations and build an aligned team.

And that one change is this: teams need to pay attention to what's happening right here and right now.

That means team members are not drifting off in the future with its hopes and fears. They are not catapulted back into the past with its nostalgia and regret. They're not trying to make the present moment into something other than what it is.

When team members can keep their attention right here and right now, seeing things just as they are without judgments, the team

can overcome distractedness and pay attention to what is
important. Team members can break down tribal barriers, stay
connected, and collaborate. They can identify assumptions, avoid
jumping to conclusions and make good decisions.[8] They can
notice reactivity and stay resilient in the face of challenges. In the
present moment and without judgments, they can meet each
other, see what is really so, and do what needs to be done. In
short, they can stay aligned.

Getting teams aligned by building their capacity to pay attention:
that's what this book is all about.

"Paying attention" and "mindfulness"

The concept of paying attention in this book is profoundly
influenced by contemporary secular mindfulness practice,
as taught by teachers such as Jon Kabat-Zinn and Sharon
Salzberg.[9] But I've chosen to use the phrase "paying
attention" rather than "mindfulness" to describe the core
experience of noticing the present moment without
judgments. The main reason for that is that "paying
attention" is more directly tied to the business outcome of
team alignment that is my focus. They say that "people
don't by drills...they buy holes." The varieties of practice
that lead to stable attention (including mindfulness
practice) constitute the drill; stable attention is the hole.

HOW TO USE THIS BOOK
The Six Steps to Better Attention

Building habits with micropractices.

The purpose of this book is to help teams deliver better results and experience more happiness as they do it. The examples and stories in this book come primarily from the world of cross-functional technology teams—the world I know and love and most want to help. Most of the concepts and practices will be effective for any team, and in any organization large or small. Specific practices can be adapted slightly as needed.

If you are a technology executive

Read this book and use it to help you pay better attention. Use it with your leadership team and your direct reports. Give the book to your program and project managers for whom it was written, have them read it, and support them in helping their teams get better results by paying better attention.

If you are a technology team leader

If you have the crucial and sometimes ill-defined role of getting people to work together (project manager, program manager, product manager, product owner, Scrum master, dev manager, etc.), then this book was written for you. Use it to improve your own ability to pay attention. Convince your leaders to support you in helping your teams learn to pay attention. Then use your influence-without-authority to do just that.

If you are an individual contributor

No matter what your role on your team, if you improve your ability to pay attention, your team's performance will improve. Remember that you have more influence than you might think.

If you don't work with technology

Working collaboratively—no matter what the context—relies on the ability of you and your team to pay attention. You may have to do just a bit of translation here and there, but virtually everything between these covers is ultimately about being human. Its lessons apply to everyone!

The process

As you'll soon see, the practice of paying attention is simple. But as any student in a French cooking school learning to make the perfect omelet can tell you, "simple" does not necessarily mean "easy." For the human brain, "simple" can actually be very challenging. We humans adore complexity (and none more so than technology-oriented humans). What follows is a process for keeping it simple, with enough details to keep brains sufficiently busy.

Choose your domain of attention

Any team can cultivate the habits of alignment by applying the basic practice of paying attention in four domains. What you want to focus on depends on your team's needs. It's recommended that you start with Chapter One, since that provides the foundation for the other chapters.

- In Chapter One, you'll learn how to stabilize your attention with the core practice of **present-moment, non-judgmental awareness**. This stabilization is exactly what you and your team need to overcome distractedness and build the habit of stable attention.
- In Chapter Two, you'll learn how to **pay attention to the people you work with**, so you can overcome tribalism and build the habit of connectedness.
- In Chapter Three, you'll learn how to **pay attention to your assumptions and presuppositions**, so you can overcome cognitive bias and build the habit of open-mindedness.

- In Chapter Four, you'll learn how to **pay attention to your emotions**, so you can overcome reactivity and build the habit of self-awareness.

The Six-Step Plan

Once you have decided on one or more domains of attention that you want to cultivate, use this seven-step plan to understand it, and then turn it into a habit.

1. Embrace the paradox

2. Find your motivation

3. Understand the obstacles

4. Understand the core practice

5. Build the habit

6. Keep it relevant

Step One: Embrace the paradox

The paradox we'll come back to over and over again in this book is that the desirable habits of team alignment do not come from trying harder. Trying harder is what causes distraction, and tribalism, and cognitive bias, and reactivity in the first place. In each instance, the remedy is to pause, and not to push. To step back, and not to lean in. To relax, and not to bear down. That's not to say that pushing, and leaning in, and bearing down don't have their place. They do...once your team is aligned. But to get aligned, and to stay aligned, takes a different kind of effort. Without question, it is not easy to pause when the pressure is on. It feels like "work" — and it is. But it's work of a different and possibly unfamiliar kind. That's the rich paradox that will recur throughout this book. Each chapter begins by reminding you of that.

Step Two: Find your motivation

The best way to develop the habit of paying attention is to find motivation. Where can you find it? On any team, each person's motivation for change will be different. Perhaps the potential satisfaction of working together in harmony is appealing. Perhaps the atmosphere of your team is just too painful to be tolerated any longer. Maybe your organization is growing, or fighting off competitive pressures, or seeking to fulfill its purpose in a more effective way. Maybe you have a different motivation that lies entirely outside of work. The stronger and more intrinsic your motivation to improve your ability to pay attention, the more easily you will acquire that habit and use it to make your team more effective.

Though identifying your motivation is mostly up to you, the **business fable** woven through the chapters may help. This narrative represents, in fictionalized form, much of what I've lived through and witnessed working in tech organizations as a team member. The experiences of the characters, and the challenges they face, may remind you of what it feels like when your team goes off the rails and inspire you to do the work to make some changes. If you are already motivated by your own drama, so much the better!

Step Three: Understand the obstacles

Acquiring the habit of paying attention is made easier by understanding what stands in the way. You can make a trip through an isolated wilderness without a trail map—but it's a lot easier if you have one. Understanding the wilderness of your own mind before you set out on a journey to develop new habits is also important. With that in mind, in the chapters ahead we'll look closely at the survival optimizations and the **brain science** that helps explain them.

Step Four: Understand the core practice

Just like learning a musical instrument or a new sport, you learn the habit of paying attention by consistently practicing it. Practicing actually changes your brain. This is due to the phenomenon of neuroplasticity. When you change your patterns of thought and behavior, your brain connections are rewired into new patterns. The wonderful German word "Trampelpfad" (a path created by people walking along the same trail in the woods) helps explain this. Suppose you set an intention to stop sending annoyed replies to the inflammatory emails a business colleague sends, seemingly every day. Your habitual behavior of responding right away is like a well-travelled path through the woods: the email comes, and you fire off a response. When you set an intention to change the pattern, it takes a deliberate effort at first, like bushwhacking your way through the underbrush. You actively refrain from responding, but you have to really think about it and resist temptation. The next time, the going is a little easier. Eventually that path is well-established…a Trampelpfad that helps you hold off on responding until you've had a chance to think through what you want to say. And the old, reactive path you sought to abandon, now no longer in use, starts to develop its own underbrush.[10]

Not every part of the brain changes in this way, and some parts are easier to change than others, but neuroplasticity means it's no longer possible for humans to make the argument "I was just born that way." If you engage in practices that lead you to think and act differently, then thinking and acting differently does get easier. The **core practice** in each chapter points to a new path through the forest to establish and develop. There are any number of specific techniques you can use to trample this path (that's what the micropractices are for), but the core practice makes it clear where you are headed.

Step Five: Build the habit

Equipped with motivation and understanding, you are ready to put the core practice to work in the context of your life, your workplace, and your team. It's time to take action!

Choose micropractices

Dopamine is the brain chemical that makes you feel good. Scientists have shown they can get rats to do just about anything by offering them dopamine as a reward.[11] Makers of games and slot machines understand that really well,[12] and we can learn a thing or two from the vast amount of research they have done to get you to spend money. What they've found, most importantly, is that the most powerful way to get someone to keep doing something is to provide rewards in very small increments. This is why games have gazillions of levels and achievements, and slot machines have smallish but rewarding payouts. If a game gives you a big dopamine hit (so satisfying!) you'll just want to go to sleep. If you get a small dopamine hit, you'll want more. (Please. Right away.)

And so, in order to develop your ability to pay attention, it's most effective to establish small, achievable goals and give yourself a lot of credit when you accomplish them. The **micropractices** in this book (and the other practices on my website, www.jhanderson.biz) are little things you can do easily and repeatedly. They might seem ridiculously small-scale, but that's exactly the point. That's how you experience satisfaction and keep coming back for more. And when it comes to building habits, coming back for more is what it's all about.

For each domain of attention there are several micropractices you can use to reinforce, contextualize, and expand the core practice of paying attention. All the micropractices have their distinctive value, but they fall into three rough categories: practices that you can do on your own; practices for you to do in your work environment; and practices for you and your team to do together. All the practices are highly adaptable, and you should feel free to make adjustments and use them in any way that works best.

Practices for you on your own

Doing individual practices is like going to an archery range. The targets are clear and stationary, there are no distractions, and there are no dangers: just you and the practice, in your own time and in your own way. There's a good reason people use archery ranges and batting cages and rehearsal studios to work out the details of their technique. With a controlled environment and a limited number of variables, it's easier to build a good foundation. Individual practices prepare you for improving your attention in the workplace and with your team, where distraction and stress are higher.

Practices for you in the workplace

At some point you have to take what you're practicing on your own and apply it in the context where it needs to be used. When you go from the archery range to the field, the target doesn't stay still, the weather may not cooperate, the bowstring gets damp and your feet get sore from tramping through the brush. This doesn't feel like the practice range at all. It's a dynamic environment, with more variables and even a bit of danger potentially lurking. All that can lead to reduced focus and attention. It takes some patience and perseverance to keep working with the bow and the arrows, letting yourself make the rookie mistakes that would never have happened during practice.

Though the workplace environment is familiar enough, it may feel quite new and strange to bring skills like self-awareness and open-mindedness into the challenging meetings and uncomfortable exchanges that are part of your work life. As with any other skill, your first attempts to apply them in the swirling chaos and pressure of the work environment may be less effective than you'd like. But as with any other skill, the key is to forgive yourself, let go, and try again. This is a form of practice too—not as controlled, not as predictable, and for a while not as effective as what you've developed on your own. Still, it does get better over time.

Practices for your team

Learning to pay attention together with your team is the most challenging set of practices, as it requires members to find common ground within their diversity. Finding agreement about changes in behavior and attitude is demanding—yet it's also fascinating. As valuable as the individual practices are, improving your attention together has the greatest potential for getting you truly and effectively aligned in powerful and lasting ways.

Doing practices together as a team is a bit like going out on a military campaign as a unit of archers. You need to work together, and there's less freedom of movement and choice than you have on your own. The practice you've done on your own is definitely relevant and will make your team function better. But you can't just pay attention to the basics of drawing back the bowstring and aiming the arrow. You need to be aware of and adjust your actions, based on the people around you and what they are doing. You also need to be aware of your collective objective, and the strategy and tactics you need to use together to accomplish that.

While the practices for yourself on your own and at work are based on individual choice and style, the practices for your team need to be consciously agreed upon as a group to improve your alignment.

Because practices are collective, and because circumstances are always changing, finding a set of practices that is authentic, effective, and grounded in the team's identity requires commitment. Just like any other team performance improvement initiative (like Lean or Agile), it's an ongoing process of discovery, adjustment, and continuous improvement. Since the focal point of the practices is present-moment awareness, experiments and modifications can happen very quickly and with minimal cost.

A few suggestions:

- If several team members (or even one) are building the habits of paying attention, the whole team's performance is likely to improve. You might start by having a few team members agree to adopt individual practices for a period of time and share with the team their discoveries of how their attention has shifted.
- In order to persist, the practices need to be relatively brief (five minutes a day or ten minutes a week can work

wonders), directly related to the work at hand, and targeted to the specific challenges the team faces.

- An important team milestone is a very good time to introduce practices associated with paying attention. This could be the initial formation/kickoff phase of a team's work, a major retrospective, or even a major point of failure that initiates a period of self-reflection. Team-building offsites are also appropriate, though it's always important to weave the practices into day-to-day work.

Build habits

Once you're chosen the micropractices you want to adopt, follow these four rules to turn them into habits.

1. Engage in the practice for a sustained period. Consider using these milestones:

   One week (for practices you do daily), or **three weeks** (for practices such as team meetings you do less frequently). That's enough time to notice the beginnings of a shift in your experience. If the practice isn't quite working for you at that point, try making modifications, or switch to a different practice.

   Sixty days. That's how much time your brain needs to achieve a level of "automaticity" where you are no longer thinking about doing the practice; you are just doing it.[13] Sixty days also gives you enough time to really evaluate the impact of the practice. If that seems like a long time, consider the duration of the last change management initiative you were involved in. Once you step back from the hypnotic urgency of the day-to-day, sixty days is not a long period for implementing a lasting change that fundamentally shifts your relationship with your work.

One year. When you have done a practice through all the seasons of the year, with the changes of weather, the holidays, and the seasonal business cycle, then it's truly yours.

2. Celebrate every little success, every little moment of recaptured attention, with unreasonable enthusiasm, so your whole brain and body get the idea you are making important shifts. See the practice **Pay Attention to the Good** on page 174 for more about the value of celebration.

3. Keep as consistent as possible. Flexibility, creativity, and freedom are wonderful, but when you're establishing a new habit leverage the power of discipline.

4. If you miss one iteration of a practice, be kind to yourself. But don't miss the next iteration.

Step Six: Keep it relevant

The last and most important part of this book is not something written on its pages: it's the way you and your team apply this material to your unique circumstances. At the end of each chapter are specific suggestions about how to do that. Those sections explore how paying attention makes a variety of business practices and methods better and more effective. The book includes a range of practices for technology teams and business teams, leaders and strategists—but even if you're not using those specific methods, I hope you will apply the principles to whatever you are working on.

Another very important way to keep the book relevant to your circumstances is to apply it to your own unique organizational culture. Having worked with technology teams in all kinds of contexts for decades, I am acutely aware of the many different flavors of team culture. My aim in this book is always to start from a place of respect for individual autonomy and team diversity, as well as the powerful ethic of independence and self-reliance that makes the tech environment such an amazing place to work in. But the truth is that the days of the cowboy freelance developer are just about over. Business and technology environments have grown too complex for teams to function effectively without a serious commitment to collaboration. The challenge for all of us is to embrace the habits of aligned teams—which means better management of some fundamental things about ourselves—while still celebrating freedom and individuality.

The specific behavioral change recommendations I make in this book are not moral judgments, but ways to improve team performance. Adopting these habits does not make you a different person. It just helps you conduct yourself differently—and more effectively—in a team context.

The third way to keep your practices local and relevant is to continuously evaluate them. As mentioned above, once you've settled on a practice it's very valuable to spend sixty days with it to form habits, consider what you are learning, and notice how things are changing. After sixty days, make necessary adjustments. Modify practices. Add practices. Choose a new domain of attention to explore.

Ultimately, the way you and your team get motivated, adopt micropractices, and reinforce the behavior you want to change, will be specific to each individual, on each team, in each organization. This diversity is inevitable. Embrace it and find the path that works for you!

CHAPTER 1
Stable Attention

Soften your gaze and stabilize your focus.

Teams with stable attention stay clear about what's important and act together to address it—even when work pressures or external distractions arise. To cultivate stable attention, practice present-moment, non-judgmental awareness, so you can overcome the inherent instability and busy-ness of the human thought-stream.

STEP ONE: EMBRACE THE PARADOX

The paradox of relaxed awareness

"Shake hands with the club," my Dad said. He was attempting, one more time, to give me a golf lesson. "Keep your right arm straight! Keep your head down! Keep your hands low! Follow through! And JUST RELAX!"

My father loved golf and played it for decades. But the sport never took with me. I think it might have been the detailed instructions he gave me every time I was preparing to take a swing. That last instruction ("JUST RELAX") was especially hard.

It is a paradox of playing golf that relaxation—stepping back from trying to focus too intently—leads to success. In many other pursuits, the same principle applies. Theatrical improvisation. Jazz improvisation. Basketball. Pottery. Martial arts. And it is no different with collaborative teams. When there is deadline pressure, things are breaking, and tensions are rising, relaxation seems counter-productive. Instead, many teams are inclined to "Bear down! Work harder! Take fewer breaks! GET FOCUSED!"

But bearing down actually reduces your ability to stay stable and focused in the present moment. When you try to stabilize your attention, your attention wobbles. Attention stabilizes when you can take a breath, step back, and observe what's going on in the moment.

STEP TWO: FIND YOUR MOTIVATION

Stable attention and your team

What makes some teams able to stay focused and productive when they are confronted with pressure or distractions, while others fall into dysfunctional patterns of panicked urgency or lack of focus? The key is the ability to get disentangled from distractions and **observe what's happening right here and right now**. Attentive teams choose to face their task list—no matter how long or urgent it is—with an inquisitive and experimental mindset: "I wonder how we might work through this and find the most important thing to focus on?" They observe distracting circumstances with interest and an open mind—then let them go or bring them into focus as appropriate. They stay open to each other, noticing their reactions to the intensity, and work together to remain in alignment. The pressure's not going to let up, and the distracting circumstances won't stop coming…but the team's ability to maintain awareness of the present moment isn't going away either. The habit is available week after week, and not just in those rare moments when circumstances line up just right.

In short, an aligned team has **the habit of stable attention**.

What is your team's current capacity for paying attention? What would be the impact of improving your focus, so you can all see clearly what is needed and keep working together despite distractions?

The Cross-Functional Team

Terra Erdman collapses into her desk chair and contemplates the Ceres Project timeline with a sigh. "Herding cats," she thinks. "Why did I think I wanted to manage this mess?"

She looks at her notes from this morning's cross-functional team meeting. An underlined comment reads, "Still need George's feedback on the new design." George Gartner, the manager of customer success at the data analytics firm Terra works for, is crucial to the Ceres Project's success. When the project kicked off six months ago, George and his team were excited about the new customer support interface. "But now," Terra thinks, "it seems like George has lost interest." She knows George is busy—that's why he spent the cross-functional meeting hunched over his laptop typing furiously in chat rooms and on email threads, helping his team through their struggles with the current antiquated customer support system. "It's ironic—the new system will make things so much better. But we'll never get it done if I can't get his attention."

Terra looks at a second note from the meeting: "Padma's 'solution'?" Padma Haldar, the Ceres Project's sponsoring VP, had also been multitasking all through the meeting. As the team was wrestling with a particularly tricky technical problem, Padma looked up from her spreadsheet briefly, threw out a solution...and then turned her attention back to her spreadsheet as though the problem was settled. "Too bad it's budget season," Terra thinks. "Maybe Padma would have thought that idea through before she blurted it out." Of course, no one was going to contradict a leader with Padma's authority and experience. Terra is pretty sure the solution is not workable, and now the whole technical team will be spending a good part of the afternoon finding that out.

And then there was this meeting note: "Need Li Hua to make database decision." Li Hua Fong, an excellent software engineer who was recently promoted to manager, has been struggling with the new role. Li Hua is greatly missing her well-respected predecessor, who has recently left the company. All through the meeting her eyes kept searching the room, apparently longing for a senior technical leader who could make the tough technical choices to appear. "She needs to stop hoping someone else will take responsibility for the decisions she has to make, or we're in real trouble," Terra thinks.

"Herding cats." While Terra was focused on keeping her team together, the people she most needed to be in sync—George, Padma, and Li Hua—were each focused on something else. When Padma offered her solution (which even Terra could see was ridiculously simplistic), Li Hua looked dazed (apparently hoping the former development manager would somehow magically reappear), and George was silent, troubleshooting a problem in a chat room. When, later in the meeting, Li Hua had raised concerns about her team's workload, Padma was busy with her spreadsheet, and George was silent—probably focused on another problem. Whenever Terra tried to engage the team in a conversation about some upcoming delivery dates that were in jeopardy...George was silent, Padma was working on her spreadsheet,

and Li Hua was looking out the window with a frown and a furrowed brow.

"Everyone is working so hard, they hardly have room to breathe," Terra thinks. "But if we're going to deliver the Ceres project, I need my team to pay attention."

That night, Terra has a hard time falling asleep, feeling annoyed with the team and all their distractedness. And at 4am she wakes up in a sweat, ruminating on the Ceres Project. Just like every day this week. "OK, this is ridiculous," she thinks. "It's not just the team that's distracted. Look at me: I'm a mess. It's like the oxygen masks on airplane flights. The parent has to put the mask on first before taking care of their kids. If I can't breathe, how can I expect my team to?"

Breathing. What was her friend and co-worker Alice telling her about learning to breathe? Wasn't it at the mindfulness class their company offers? "Hmm," Terra thinks. "A class to teach me how to breathe. Bizarre. But I need to do something."

STEP THREE: UNDERSTAND THE OBSTACLES

The busy brain

Busy and distracted thinking is a part of our human evolutionary heritage. Our brains were formed in ancestral landscapes full of dangers. In that environment, survival was the first priority. Avoiding saber-tooth tigers and tracking down delicious purple berries kept us busy for thousands of years. Like all creatures, we needed to pay close attention to the threats and opportunities all the time. If your attention wasn't constantly scanning the surrounding bushes, checking for danger, checking for resources, you probably wouldn't last long.

The attentional spotlight

There are several models for the complex brain science of attention.[14] One useful model compares your faculty of paying attention to a spotlight, moving sequentially to highlight one object after another. A refinement of this model is the zoom-lens model. As your attention zooms in, your area of focus gets smaller but you see more detail. Underlying the various models is the principle of "allocation of resources": there's only so much attentional capacity you have. If you're surrounded by survival-related needs, then attentional scanning is the way to go.

We're in a different environment today, but the inclination of the attentional spotlight to move rapidly is still with us. It's a natural by-product of our ancestry. And given the richly stimulating connected digital environments humans have created for themselves today, our attentional scanning is happening faster than ever.

Continual scanning has the negative consequence of creating attentional fatigue and instability. That's a problem for managing the complex needs of a collaborative team, where the ability to see with clarity is so important. When teams face challenges that require extended reflection, sustained problem-solving, and building persistent interpersonal connections, the ability to engage stable attention is a necessity.

The default mode

The inherently unstable nature of the attentional spotlight is not the only factor that makes focusing difficult. We also have to contend with an even more fundamental characteristic of our thinking, what neuroscientist Marcus Raichle identified as the "default mode."[15] The default mode is a baseline of brain activity that's going on all the time regardless of your will, the way your lungs breathe and your heart beats. The default mode plays a variety of roles, such as keeping the brain's wiring healthy and active. Its effect, though, is to provide us with a steady stream of thoughts—memories, evaluations, fantasies, predictions. And this stream goes on continually, night and day (the default mode is the source of dreaming activity).

The default mode contributes to unstable attention by distracting you from what's happening in front of you. If default mode activity is interesting enough, it grabs your attentional spotlight, easily out-prioritizing whatever might be going on in your field of awareness. The result is you become "lost in thought," no longer listening to the status meeting or catching the nuances of expression on a co-worker's face.

The thought-stream

You've got quite a busy brain: much of the time your attentional spotlight is busy hopping from one item to the next in search of survival benefits, and when that's not happening the default mode is operating. The default mode is something like a three-ring circus. There are clowns, trapeze artists, fire-eaters and

animals—a hive of activity of all sorts. The attentional spotlight is
roving the scene, picking out in turn the ringmaster, the human
cannonball, the bareback rider. When a popcorn vendor comes by
(survival benefit!) the spotlight swings there immediately. When
a particularly scary-looking clown leers at you (survival risk), the
spotlight swings there.

*Let's call the combination of these two ever-present destabilizing
factors—the obsessive and continual activity of scanning your
environment, and the equally obsessive and continual activity of
generating thoughts—your thought-stream. Your thought-stream is the
ongoing circus with its wildly panning spotlight in your mind. The
circus may be fun for a while, but if you want to stabilize your attention
you need a way to gain control over your thought-stream.*

The executive function to the rescue

In addition to the attentional spotlight and the default mode,
there is a third type of brain activity. This one is all about control:
your **executive function** (also known as cognitive control).[16] The
executive function has the potential to rescue your awareness
from the herky-jerky and obsessively busy thought-stream. As
the name suggests, the executive function is the choice-making
capability of your brain. And yet the executive function can be
overshadowed by other brain networks. Much of the time, we
choose to go along with the unstable scanning propensities of the
attentional spotlight, and why we get lost in the ongoing thought
processes of the default mode. In these circumstances the
executive function is operational but half awake, only vaguely
participating in regulating the thought-stream.

But the executive function does have the ability to wake up and make a different choice. It can begin to engage with the other brain networks in ways that stabilize attention and reduce distraction. This is not as simple as flipping a switch, since the activities of the thought-stream are habitual and powerful. To stabilize attention, **the executive function needs to develop the habit of alertness,** so it can regain attentional control.

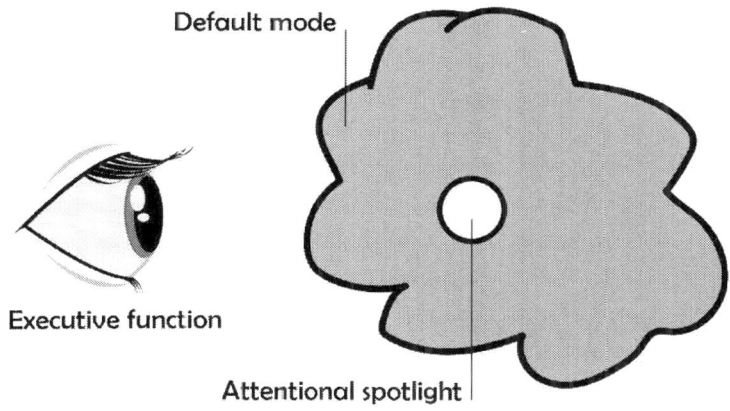

I've always found the idea that there are different parts of ourselves jockeying for control a little disconcerting. But it actually fits my recent experience very well. As a solo author and entrepreneur, I often get very wound into the particular task I'm doing (whether it's writing a book, working with clients, or business development). It's when I step back from these tasks and put on my "executive hat" that I can see more clearly the context for what I'm doing and make good decisions about my priorities.

What I've just described is rooted in recent brain science, part of the near-miraculous advances in our understanding of the mysteries of human consciousness assisted by the latest experimental and research techniques. It's quite remarkable, then, that almost 2,400 years ago, a very similar view of human consciousness was put forward by the ancient Greek philosopher Plato.

> *First the charioteer of the human soul drives a pair*
> *[of horses], and secondly one of the horses is noble*
> *and of noble breed, but the other quite the opposite*
> *in breed and character. Therefore, in our case the*
> *driving is necessarily difficult and troublesome.*[17]

Not bad, given the lack of ancient Athenian fMRI machines. While we might not subscribe to the notion of one "noble" and one "quite the opposite" horses, the image of a charioteer (aka the executive function) needing to exert influence over an unruly pair of brain activities (the default mode network and the attentional spotlight) makes the essential point: we have unstable brains, but we do also have the capacity to step back and stabilize their activity. It just takes a little skill.

Step Four: Understand the Core Practice

Notice what's happening now

There is one essential practice that trains the executive function to stay alert, so it can more effectively manage the thought-stream: the practice of **cultivating present moment, non-judgmental awareness**. Though this practice has many labels (mindfulness, centering, groundedness, presence, waking up) they are all metaphors for the core experience of paying attention to what is happening right here, right now, without desire or aversion. Regardless of the label, the aim is to find your way to a fundamentally stable experience of reality.

Experiments and Practices

Each chapter includes a few experiments to try as you read. These will give you brief experiences to help you grasp the somewhat abstract concepts I'm introducing. To turn these one-off experiences into habits, you can use the suggested daily micropractices at the end of the book. Or, you can turn the experiments themselves into daily practices if you like.

Present-moment

The first way to wake up your executive function and regain control of your thought-stream is to notice *what is happening now*. Your thought-stream, including both the attentional spotlight and the default mode, is very interested in two things: what has happened, and what is about to happen. The thought-stream uses current experience to predict what might be coming and prepare to deal with it. When it's not focused on the future, it's focused in the past, doing post-mortems on what has happened (last week, last month, or 20 years ago) and figuring out how to avoid or replicate those experiences. When you bring your attention to the present moment, the distracting power of the thought-stream retreats, and stability emerges. No matter how chaotic the present moment is, it's much more stable than the thought-stream.

Experiment: Notice Your Nose

Close your eyes and focus your attention on the tip of your nose for 30 seconds (if you breathe normally, that will be five to seven breaths). When you're done, open your eyes and keep reading.

It probably didn't take long for you to start to notice the unstable quality of your attention, as your spotlight flicked around, and your default mode manufactured its stream of thoughts. It's virtually certain that only a fraction of those 30 seconds was spent right here and right now with the tip of your nose. For that brief period, you weren't planning or worrying about the future, and you weren't ruminating on the past. For that brief period, your attention had stability.

Non-judgmental

The second way you can wake up your executive function and regain control of your thought-stream is to notice what is happening now *as it is, without judgments*. To the extent that it relates to the present at all, your thought-stream has one goal in mind: to determine whether what is happening now is a good or a bad thing. From a survival perspective, this makes a lot of sense. If something is good or desirable, you will approach it. If something is distasteful or unpleasant, you will avoid it. In various subtle ways all of your thought-stream is infused with judgment. When you actively refrain from judgment, you're taking away one of the key nutrients that feeds the thought-stream's distracting power.

Experiment: Quick Body Scan

Close your eyes and scan your body for a place that is uncomfortable right now—any little twinge or itch or ache will do. For 30 seconds (5 to 7 breaths), notice this sensation, just as it is. When you're done, open your eyes and keep reading.

It's likely three things happened during the 30 seconds. Much of the time your thought-stream was busy flickering here and there in its usual fashion. Some of the time you experienced the discomfort as something unpleasant you

wanted to resist or found distasteful (a need to stretch or
shift, a worrisome question as to whether you need to go
to the dentist, work out more, eat less). And, for some
small fraction of the time, you just noticed the sensation,
without making judgments or evaluations. You were
actually experiencing what was happening, just as it was
in the moment. And in that moment your attention
became more stable.

Awareness

Your thought-stream and the rest of your experience comprise
one unified and integrated field of consciousness. Waking up
your executive function does not require you to distance yourself
from your thought-stream, or to shut it down. You're just gently
including it in a larger context. That context includes sensory
input, body sensations, emotions, aesthetic experience and more.
Attending to these other aspects of experience outside your
thought-stream is a very good way to come back to present-
moment, non-judgmental awareness, and is a key to many of the
specific practices in this book.

Experiment: Listen

Close your eyes and, for 30 seconds, listen for the quietest
sound you can hear right now. When you're done, open
your eyes and keep reading.

Regardless of your acoustic environment, you probably
noticed a couple of things during those 30 seconds. Your
thought-stream was busily at work and consumed much
of your attention. But, for the portion of time when you
were really listening, you gradually began to hear more
and more sounds. At first you might have heard the loud
conversation in the next cube over, or a plane flying
overhead. But slowly, like the ripples spreading out on the
surface of a pond, your ears began to get more engaged
with progressively smaller sonic details. The tick of a
clock, the hum of a fan, or distant footsteps started to
come into focus. However briefly, you began to get a
sense that your thought-stream is happening within a
spacious world full of interesting activity. And by putting
your thoughts in a larger context, even briefly and to a
small degree, your attention stabilized.

Two images of stable attention

It's important to have a conceptual understanding of the idea of
present-moment, non-judgmental awareness. But some
metaphors can also help the brain get out of its own way.

The target: The first metaphor draws on the world of archery. We can visually represent "present-moment, non-judgmental" as occupying a space beyond the dualities of the past-future continuum and the good-bad continuum. When your attention is present right now and without judgments, it's like focusing on the bullseye of a target.

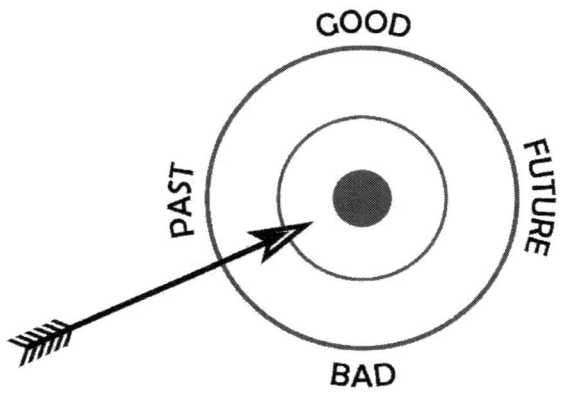

Experiment: The Target

Repeat the first exercise of noticing your nose for 30 seconds. This time, pay attention to how your mind wanders: does it drift off into the past, remembering what happened an hour ago, or a year ago? Does it go into the future, worrying or hoping that something will or won't happen? Does it try to push away an unpleasant thought or sensation, or lean in with longing for something it desires? When your attention moves away from the bullseye of the present moment, gently bring it back.

The mountain: The second metaphor comes from the natural world. Nature metaphors seem to make it a bit easier for the mind to step back from its incessant busy-ness and stabilize its attention. Maybe that's because the brain evolved to operate best when it's out-of-doors and feels more at home with natural imagery.[18]

Experiment: The Mountain

Close your eyes and visualize a large mountain. Take a moment to notice its beauty, its massive size and weight, and—above all—its stability. Now, imagine yourself taking on the mountain's attributes. Spend 30 seconds just noticing, with curiosity, what that's like. Feel your weight settling into the ground. Feel your solidity. Continue to breathe naturally, while you sit, very stable and grounded. When thoughts start to arise, imagine them as being like the wind blowing, or clouds drifting by. Meanwhile, your awareness remains stable, and grounded, and rooted in the earth.

Core Practice: Pay attention

As with any habit, you can develop the habit of stable attention through practice. The basic practice of staying right here and right now to cultivate stable attention is very simple—as simple as the experiments you just did. If we do a little process analysis, each of those experiments has these steps:

1. The first step is the most important: make a commitment to stabilize your attention with the steps that follow. Establish a timeframe for the practice. It could be as short as 30 seconds, or 2 minutes, or 5 minutes or longer.

2. Choose an object in your field of awareness. This can be literally anything: physical sensations, sensory input, an item in your environment, or even something you imagine.

3. Set an intention to focus on that object without judgments in the present moment.

4. Focus your attention on the object for a brief period of time (as little as 30 seconds, or a few minutes, or longer if you wish).

5. When your attention wanders away, bring it back, gently and without judgments.

6. Reset your intention and repeat.

7. When you finish the session, notice what's changed. How has the stability of your attention shifted?

That's the core practice. The micropractices referenced below give you specific contexts for working with this practice. The details will vary a bit, but the fundamental practice is the same.

STEP FIVE: BUILD THE HABIT

Cultivating the habit of stable attention

You can improve your ability to bring stable attention to your work—and bring that same ability to your team. Choose one or more of these micropractices and do it every day. See page 17 for more about building habits.

What to expect as you build the habit

Since the thought-stream is designed to work the way it does (busy, unstable, shooting off into the past and future, making judgments), you won't be able to shut it down, or even change its behavior. The goal is to become relatively less victimized by the shenanigans of the thought-stream, by expanding the context. What you'll experience with these practices may not feel like much of a difference: occasional moments of clarity, bracketed by ferocious bouts of thinking. That's OK: **recovering from distraction (step 5 above) is the most important part of the process.** The shift is that your thought-stream is not 100% in control. Even if it's now 98% in control, that 2% is enough of a wedge to start changing your relationship with distraction and to begin to develop stable attention, on your own, in your workplace and with your team.

The Cross-Functional Team (continued)

*In the company's mindfulness class Terra learns to do a simple
breathing practice. (Micropractice: Pay Attention to Your Breath)
Surprisingly, even just a few minutes of bringing her attention to her
breath seems to cause her thoughts to slow down just the tiniest bit.
And though she would not describe herself as "calm" after the exercise,
it does seem that her thinking has gotten a bit clearer. It makes enough
of a difference that she decides to do the practice in the car for two
minutes every morning before she turns on the ignition.*

*As the launch date gets closer, the stresses of the Ceres Project are
taking their toll. Although Terra is now more relaxed as she starts her
day, as soon as she dives into her email inbox that stability vanishes and
she's back to her normal distracted state of mind. And yet there is one
important difference: she has a taste of what stability feels like. The
ordinary everyday distractedness now feels off-kilter and ineffective.*

*One afternoon she reflects on the time she just wasted sorting through a
demand from Padma that seemed urgent at 10am and was irrelevant by
noon. Terra knows that if she'd had the presence of mind to ask Padma
the right questions in the first place, she could have saved herself that
effort. "This kind of thing happens all the time," Terra thinks. "It seems
awfully hard to find two minutes to breathe during the day. But I think
one or two breaths, here and there, would really help—if I could just
remember to do that!" (Micropractice: Find an Anchor Point)*

A couple of weeks later, with the help of her morning breathing practice and the occasional reminder to breathe during the workday, Terra finds she's making progress in getting more focused and less distracted. And it's starting to show up in her work; she's asking better questions and listening more carefully. By setting an example of grounded calm for others to follow, she's helping the whole team. Things are still crazy, but in each meeting and phone call there's just a bit more space. Terra is remembering to thank people more, and there's even a bit of laughter here and there. Li Hua has dropped by her desk to make a comment— "Whatever you're doing, things are a little better than they used to be"—before launching into a series of complaints about Padma and her unrealistic ideas.

If anything, the changes Terra is experiencing in her own attentiveness are making the distracted behavior that still shows up in team meetings even more intolerable. Encouraged by Li Hua's feedback, Terra starts to wonder how she can more directly help her team improve its attention as a group. "I'm not going to convince everyone to do what I'm doing," she thinks. "But I think we can still bring some stable attention to our meetings. It would really make a difference." She begins by making a few subtle changes to the way she runs the cross-functional team meetings—nothing dramatic, just bringing in a little more structure and intention. (Micropractice. Pay Attention in Meetings) Though it still feels like she's herding cats, there is less wasted time, and the team is less likely to walk out of the room without having made any decisions or commitments. When a conversation threatens to spiral out of control, Terra takes a breath and gets the team back to the agenda.

A few days later Terra is surprised and a little nervous when Padma calls her into her office. "Terra," Padma says, as she continues to type and stare intently at her monitor, "There's a lot of pressure to get Ceres launched. You're doing a good job—it seems like things have been running more smoothly the past few weeks. But we're still under the gun. What can I do to help us move faster?" A few weeks ago, Terra would have muttered something about everything being fine and fled the office. But now she pauses and finds just enough space to say, "Actually—I think our team wastes a lot of time because people are so distracted. What would make the most difference is if we could do something specific to, you know, improve our ability to pay attention."

Padma stops typing and looks at her. "Do you have any ideas about how we could do that—and still keep pushing ahead? We're getting down to the wire." Terra takes a breath: "I think if we can get together for a couple of hours to work on paying attention, we'll save at least that much time in a couple of weeks." "Hmm," Padma says. "I don't know how much good that will do. But OK. Two hours. I'm willing to give it a try."

Terra makes good use of the group's time. She explains the changes she's made for herself, and how that has influenced the way she runs meetings. She introduces a couple of simple exercises she's learned, like breathing and walking attentively. Finally, she proposes one simple protocol for the team to use together so they can stay focused and productive. (Micropractice: Pay Attention as a Team) "I think," she says, "if we can just notice when we're getting distracted, and find a way to recover our attention together, we'll get Ceres out the door in much better shape—and on time."

STEP SIX: KEEP IT RELEVANT

Lean and Kanban

As Terra's story illustrates, spending time cultivating your team's and your organization's ability to maintain stable attention will make any initiative go more smoothly and produce better results. Two widely used process improvement methodologies, Lean and Kanban, illustrate this beautifully.

Stable attention and Lean

Lean manufacturing is a set of practices pioneered by Toyota in the late 1940's that have been broadly adopted in many domains (auto manufacturing, healthcare, environmental, software development, and more). The goal of Lean is to reduce waste and continually improve processes, while remaining respectful of people as you do so. While Lean includes a wide variety of practices, the heart of Lean is *seeing what is so*. And that's exactly what stable attention makes possible.

Let's consider one key Lean practice as an example: walking the gemba. *Gemba* is a Japanese word that can be translated as "the real place." In Lean, it refers to "where work is done" or "where value is created."

> *Walking the gemba is a process of going to where*
> *work is being done with intent of assessing how*
> *well processes (not people) are performing,*
> *discovering what obstacles (wastes) are thwarting*
> *people, understanding the relationships between*

steps in a value stream, or uncovering root causes
of problems. [19]

The gemba could be a manufacturing floor, or a collaborative planning meeting, or a chat room—anywhere the work is being done. Walking the gemba means deliberately setting out to observe what is going on in that environment, not for the immediate purpose of making judgments or taking action, but so you can see clearly what is so. Action to improve processes will follow, but the first step is to observe.

If you haven't developed the habit of stable attention, when you set out on a gemba walk your busy brain will get the best of you. Rather than noticing what's actually happening, you'll be lost in thought: back in the past, out in the future, averse to what's not working or drawn to what is. You may come up with great ideas to reduce waste and improve your processes. But because your attention is not rooted in observing what is actually happening now, those ideas are likely to miss the mark.

If, on the other hand, you've been cultivating the habit of stable attention, you may still experience distraction as you walk the gemba. If you're under pressure to make things better, it's inevitable your attention will be drawn away from the present moment. But—and this is the key difference—you know how to recover from distraction. You can see you're distracted, take a moment to reset, and reengage with whatever you need to be looking at.

A practice for better Lean

All the Stable Attention micropractices will create more stable attention for yourself and your team, and therefore will make you a better Lean practitioner. Here's one practice that may be especially helpful:

 The next time you walk the gemba, use the Find an Anchor Point micropractice to stabilize your attention before you start. If you get distracted during the walk, come back to the anchor point and refocus before you resume.

When I was working on a large technology integration initiative for a grantee of a major philanthropic organization, the development team had a sock monkey for a mascot. Team members would randomly move the sock monkey from place to place in the cube farm. Since no-one knew where it would show up next, it functioned like an anchor point (with some humor attached)—whenever the sock monkey appeared in an unexpected location, team members would stop what they were doing and have a chuckle. The sock monkey became, in effect, an invitation to walk the gemba. More often than not, seeing the monkey created a pause—and in that pause was a reminder to step back for a moment, consider the bigger picture, and ask whether they were working as effectively as they could.

Stable attention and Kanban

Kanban, a scheduling system developed by Toyota as part of Lean manufacturing, is widely used in software development and other business processes. The practice of Kanban manages workflows by specifying stages of work, creating a limit to the number of items in each stage, and moving individual items through the stages in a structured way.

The most important thing to say about Kanban and the practice of stable attention is this: if your task list is too full to give you time to pause and step back, even just a little bit, your attention will never stabilize. If you are frantically running from one meeting to another without any pause for breath between, your attention will never stabilize. Unless you can make the decision (and find the support) to limit the items on your list so you can make stable attention a priority—your attention will never stabilize. In other words, stable attention requires that you first take note of your personal Kanban list and make a small slice of room for practicing stable attention. This practice doesn't have to be more than a few minutes a day—but if the practice isn't on your list, it's not going to happen.

When it comes to managing a Kanban board for your team, there are a lot of similarities between a well-groomed board and the psychology of stable attention. The native instability of the attentional spotlight and the default mode network correlates to an overfull and randomized task list—the normal state teams find themselves in without a Kanban. As with the limited capacity of the attentional spotlight, a team has limited capacity to focus on list items. The Kanban board, like the executive function, plays the role of providing the big picture, so the team can step back and observe the whole. It helps with making choices about what to attend to, what to hold until later, and what to let go.

To bring stable attention to your Kanban board, the first priority is to get the board to accurately represent your current reality. You might have to begin by giving up the tidiness of the board, so it can reflect the messiness of reality. By paying close attention to what is actually so, you can get the real work items, the real queues, and the real work stages on the board. Once the reality is clearly represented there, you're in a position to reflect on the whole, and start making the board more aligned with what you want.

These down-in-the-weeds tasks are powerful exercises for building stability of attention. Stable attention and a good Kanban board act as a virtuous circle. Stable attention gives you the focus to make your Kanban board more accurate. You're seeing the world more clearly, and less willing to ignore what's happening no matter how messy it is. At the same time, an accurate Kanban board—by mirroring back an accurate view of what is so—makes it harder for your attention to go wandering off.

A practice for better Kanban
You can use any of the Stable Attention micropractices to create more stable attention for yourself and your team. As a result, you'll get a Kanban board of better quality. But here's one practice that could be of particular benefit:

Use the Pay Attention as a Team micropractice when you are reviewing your Kanban board. When fatigue sets in, or someone gets impatient with stage definitions, or conversation leans toward "we'll deal with that later"—invoke the protocol. Take a brief step back as a group, spend a few seconds recovering your attention, and then decide how to proceed. This simple protocol will keep your board cleaner and your attention sharper.

When I started working with the Finance executives for a large international media company, the technology project list had dozens of items on it and conversations about priorities were a free-for-all. After some negotiation, the team agreed to gather regularly and make use of a decision-making framework for prioritizing projects. In fact, this first step of agreeing to meet periodically to work on priorities was the most important thing we did. In essence, we put stability of attention at the top of our Kanban. In the meetings we stepped back to get clarity about strategic priorities. We created a template to estimate the business value of each project. And we created and started to manage a Kanban board. The board (along with the other tools) would not have been possible if we had not found a way to stabilize our attention. And the tools helped us keep our attention stable through the inevitable shifts that occurred as we moved forward.

CHAPTER 2
Connectedness

Ease your boundaries and gain security.

Connected teams act together across organizational, cultural, and personal boundaries, even when they face challenges to cohesiveness. To cultivate connectedness, pay attention to other people with curiosity, and expand your definition of "us," so you can overcome the inherently tribal nature of the human thought-stream.

STEP ONE: EMBRACE THE PARADOX

The paradox of the tribe

When the Seahawks won the Super Bowl in 2014, I was working in an office building in Seattle's Stadium District. Though I am not a fan of big crowds, I couldn't resist joining the massive victory celebration happening later that week, just outside my window. I made my way down to King Street and found myself wedged into the most compact mass of humans I've ever been part of. The crush was by turns overwhelming, scary—and ultimately glorious, as the crowd burst into a sustained howl of tribal ecstasy as the caravan with the team (and its trophy) passed by. I'm not sure I've ever felt so whole-heartedly a part of a group.

Here's the paradox, though. By bonding with my fellow Seattleites, I was also increasing my sense of separation from the good people of Denver (whose Broncos the Seahawks had soundly defeated during the game). Tribal identity creates a great feeling while it's happening…and there's no question that humans are hard-wired to operate this way! But as satisfying as that experience of connectedness can be, it won't work when you need to reach out across tribal boundaries. In work contexts where complex collaboration across multiple teams is a requirement, tribal bonds work against you. You need a different kind of connectedness, one that extends beyond your group's boundaries, and results in a different and wider definition of "us."

STEP TWO: FIND YOUR MOTIVATION

Connectedness and your team

Why can some teams remain in synch when pressure and changes come, while others get stuck in tribalism, conflict, or fragmentation? It's easier if teams have good "chemistry"—but that is not the primary factor. Regardless of diverse personalities or backgrounds, when teams choose to see and interact with each other as human beings, they will flourish. The indispensable skill needed to make this happen is an ability to **pay attention *to each other* right here and right now**. Not just at team-building events, but even when—especially when—the pressure is on. Aligned teams pay attention to each other, listen to each other, and understand each other. They embrace new team members and reach out to build relationships with the other teams they're working with. They connect with new leaders, and new leaders connect with them. When misunderstandings arise, they actively address them, right away. If something in a relationship doesn't seem right, they ask about each other about it, not relying on assumptions. They negotiate the changes and challenges together, and although it's tough they get the job done on time.

In short, an aligned team has **the habit of connectedness**.

How well do your team members collaborate with each other and with outside groups? What would be the impact of strengthening your network of human relationships, so you can keep talking and working together, even when there are challenges?

The Incident

Terra takes a taste of warm champagne from a plastic cup. It's surprisingly delicious, but maybe that's because of the context: the team has released the Ceres Project customer service functionality. The team's newfound habit of maintaining stable attention (using the simple protocol Terra introduced) has helped. Despite the inevitable late-night crunch toward the end, she's heard from several people that the launch was unusually smooth. As Terra looks with satisfaction at the subdued, somewhat awkward group gathered for their little launch party, George, the customer success manager, strolls over to Terra munching a Ceres Project Launch cookie.

"I'm concerned." he says. "My team didn't get a chance to do as much testing as I wanted. I hope this doesn't come back to bite us. We're busy enough as it is."

After George saunters off, Li Hua, the development manager, appears by Terra's side. "I heard what he said," she whispers. "Does he not remember all the test cases we sent his team that they never completed?" Terra sips her champagne reflectively but doesn't respond. She has the same concern. "Oh well," she thinks. "I'll enjoy the party while I can."

It doesn't take long for Terra's anxiety to be validated. Within a week of launch, George's customer success team runs into a thicket of problems with the system. Unfortunately, he is too busy helping his team deal with angry customers to keep attending Ceres Project team meetings.

His team is getting more and more frustrated about the problems, and finally George insists that they get direct access to the data in the Ceres database, bypassing the user interface Li Hua's team has built.

Li Hua is annoyed by this move, and also more than a little worried about what George's team might do to the data in the system. "We built that interface for a reason — to preserve the integrity of the data," she tells Terra. But her developers have a new project to work on that is already late, and in any case, she's not getting much information from George's team about what the specific issues are. After a long and contentious phone call with George, she reluctantly agrees to give his team access. George is content, and the situation calms down, but at a cost: an invisible wall starts to form between the two groups. Everyone agrees Terra has been doing a great job keeping the team focused during meetings. But the data episode contributes to the centrifugal force of conflict. In the tone of emails and conversations — and the conversations that aren't happening — Terra can see evidence that the team is starting to fall apart.

Padma, the sponsoring executive, would be able to help break down the barriers between groups, but she's got issues of her own. Terra doesn't have many details but knows that Padma and Carlos, the company's CIO and Padma's boss, are spending a lot of time in closed-door meetings full of executives.

Clearly Padma is distracted and has actually snapped at Terra irritably a time or two. "That's not what I'd expect from Padma," Terra thinks. "I wonder what's going on." Ceres seems to be the last thing Padma wants to be thinking about.

Late one Friday afternoon Terra gets an email from Padma: "I'm sorry Terra, but the project has launched, and everyone has to move on. I really need Li Hua to be working on something else, and George can handle his own team's issues. I want you to keep working with Li Hua's team on fixing the Ceres bugs, but George is going to step back from team meetings. And I am too."

The customer success team stays up late manually entering data, apologizing to customers, and grumbling. The development team fixes a few issues but has largely moved on to new work. The executive team is consumed with…whatever it is they are talking about in those closed-door conference rooms.

"How frustrating," Terra thinks. "Breaking up the team—not the best way to fix the Ceres Project problems." She sighs. "I bet Padma has given in to pressure from George. He's just not very interested in collaborating." In the meantime, although her own work responsibilities are in flux, she continues with her daily practices. As frustrating as the situation is, keeping her attention stable is always helpful.

And then, late the following Friday, a phone call wakes Terra up. "Terra, this is Li Hua. It looks like Ceres just crashed. The database got corrupted—I warned George his team's workarounds were going to cause problems. Looks like I was right."

All weekend, the Ceres Project team reconvenes in a series of very long calls and chat sessions to coordinate the work of communications to angry customers, recovering as much lost data as possible, and fixing the biggest user interface issues that led to the workarounds in the first place. Both Padma and Carlos join the calls regularly. Under the

pressure and urgency of the situation, the team's esprit de corps
revives. Terra keeps the team focused and moving forward, reminding
them from time to time to recover their attention when it starts to flag.
Li Hua and George put aside their differences and work closely together,
along with their teams, to sort out some tricky details of timing. The
executives make quick decisions when they are needed and stay closely
connected with the whole team. By the end of the weekend, as the triage
reaches completion, there's a giddy sense of accomplishment…even as
everyone dreads the post-mortem meeting where their collective
weaknesses will be exposed. Late Sunday Terra gets a note from Padma:
"Terra, you need to get those cross-functional team meetings for Ceres
going again. I can see that we broke up the group a little too quickly. I'll
make sure everyone understands how important that is."

This isn't the first time Terra has seen a crisis weld a fragmented group
of individuals into a coordinated unit. They were lucky to have found
and fixed the problem so quickly. But she knows the crisis could have
been avoided if her team had been working together better all along.

She wonders, "Do we really need to stay up all night fixing a crisis to
find common ground and work together? There must be a better way for
us to stay more in synch day to day—even when individual needs and
priorities don't line up."

After the tough weekend, Terra takes Monday off. On a long walk at the
lake with her dog Rex, she wonders what it would take to keep her team
connected so they can work together more effectively. "It's been a while
since we all went out to lunch together. I'll see if Padma has some funds
for that."

STEP THREE: UNDERSTAND THE OBSTACLES

The tribal brain

The experience of connectedness with other people is not easy to achieve. To see why, let's go back to the ancestral savannah.

Avoiding social danger

We humans were poorly equipped to survive in that dangerous and unprotected environment. No fangs, no claws, hardly any protective fur. Not that fast, or big, or strong. The only reason we were able to survive those early days and make it into the present is that we became very good at cooperation. On your own, you didn't have much chance of survival. And getting kicked out of the tribe was one of the very worst things that could happen to you.

The danger didn't just come from saber-tooth tigers. We humans have been a pretty violent species: something like 2% of all deaths in prehistory came from human-on-human violence (today it's around 0.006%).[20] Having a good strong tribe around you to keep you safe from the threat of other tribes was essential. And when something went wrong for you socially within your tribe, the consequences could be just as lethal.

As I'm writing this in July 2018, the World Cup in Russia is under way. A recent *New York Times* article discusses the characteristic gesture soccer players make when they miss an easy shot on goal: they put their hands on their heads.[21] It turns out that this is the same behavior other primates exhibit when they have done something shameful. The gesture communicates: "Don't hurt me.

Don't exclude me from the group. Don't kill me." So deeply ingrained is this response to failure that blind athletes do the same thing. Whether you are a soccer player or not, you are wired to be hyper-aware of your social standing.

The original facial recognition software

Humans have astonishingly adept facial recognition capabilities. We have brain regions specifically devoted to recognizing faces and associating them with names. Beyond that, dozens of other brain regions are recruited to fill in the identification, facial expression, and semantic meaning gaps so we can instantly determine whether someone is inviting us to join the campfire circle or casting us into outer darkness.[22]

In the churn of human social interactions with their consequences for survival and acceptance, we draw additional conclusions from all sorts of facial cues. Research has shown that, across races, we rate people with skin that has a more yellowish tinge as healthier and more attractive. Faces that are wider are considered less trustworthy and more exploitative. And people with longer faces are viewed as better leaders.[23]

Another illustration of the importance of subtle human interactions is the color of our eyes. The fact that we have white around the irises of our eyes means it's very easy to spot which way someone is looking (and we really care about that!). The eyes of other primates don't have this feature (the area around the iris is black). Even among primates, we are uniquely tuned to pay attention to social relationships.[24]

This same level of sophistication is utilized by our ever-vigilant social brains as we interpret conversations, emails, chat room discussions, video conferences and other ways we interact. No matter how we communicate, we are always on high alert to ascertain whether we belong, or whether someone else belongs, driven by an ever-present built-in predisposition to notice the subtlest nuances as indicators of potential danger (being excluded from the group) or safety (being included).

Since we now live in far safer circumstances, we have transferred much of the base anxiety about social belonging to the complex overlapping identities we carry around with us. The group you work with, the organization you work for, the team you are part of, your professional role—and of course, gender, ethnicity and all the other categories that extend beyond the workplace—for all these identities, you are constantly scanning for where you belong and where you don't belong, assessing where the danger is and where the safety is. It's exhausting! But it also helps explain why people often struggle to find their place when they join a new team. There are a lot of competing identities to take care of. Our system is wired to be on the lookout for social danger. The stakes feel high.

Feeling good together

Avoiding social danger is not the only motivation for our tribal tendencies, though. We don't just bond with others because it's scary out there. We bond because it's emotionally satisfying. For example, the hormone oxytocin is released when we do social things like cuddle with a loved one, play with the dog, or sing together. Oxytocin makes you feel good and heightens the experience of connectedness with your tribe. At the same time, oxytocin seems to decrease connectedness with people outside the tribe and increase the likelihood of being dishonest to serve the interests of the in-group.[25] As any sports fan knows, the strength of connectedness with one's own fan base is pretty much equal to the strength of disdain (sometimes violent) one feels toward the fans of other teams.

We don't need hormone studies to know how much we value belonging to a group. We know through our experiences of schooling, work, and socializing that being included in a group feels great and being left out feels terrible. A recent study found that when participants were set up to experience feeling excluded from a game, the brain regions registering distress were the same regions that register physical pain.[26] It literally hurts to feel left out.

Theory of Mind

But let's add one more important complication to the mix: what brain scientists call "Theory of Mind." This is our ability to recognize that other people have a different point of view than we do. At a very early age we develop the ability to recognize that other people have a separate existence from us. The game of "peekaboo" works so well with very young children because they don't yet have a sense of the continuous existence of other people. When you hide from a baby, as far as the baby is concerned you have disappeared. Then "peekaboo!" there you are again, like magic. As we grow up, we quickly become more sophisticated and learn other people exist even when we don't see them. We also learn that they see the world from a different point of view. And soon we are doing much more than that: we start to construct a more detailed story about just what that point of view is.[27]

This is all quite useful and necessary, but it's easy to forget that our theories about other people's minds are just that—theories. We begin to think we have an accurate view of how others see the world, based solely on our interpretation of what we can see. But if anyone ever thought you were mad at them when in fact you were just coming down with a cold, you know interpretations can be seriously wrong. If you ever concluded that someone on another team was lazy or incompetent until you found out that their partner has been battling cancer, you know your Theory of Mind can be full of holes.

STEP FOUR: UNDERSTAND THE CORE PRACTICE

Pay attention to other people

How can you develop habits that will enable you to relate to your co-workers effectively, despite the unmistakable presence of all this neurological baggage? How do you stay connected— especially across team boundaries—when you're facing a powerful system that reinforces tribal boundaries through rewards like hug-generated oxytocin and punishments like exclusion-associated physical pain and missed-goal shame? How can you fine-tune your hypersensitive facial recognition circuits?

How can you continually update your Theory of Mind about the people you work with, so you're seeing them as accurately as possible, rather than through the filter of your own assumptions?

The answer to all these questions is the same: pay attention!

When other people are around, the thought-stream gets busy with references to the past and future (for example, nostalgia for the way the team used to be or anxiety about where it is headed). Desire and aversion are stimulated by hard-wired concerns about inclusion and exclusion. Your Theory of Mind is busy supplying you with a set of judgments about who each person in the room is, and what they want. Staying right here, right now in the moment with a group of people takes some practice! But the habit of stable attention introduced in Chapter One provides the foundation you can use to stay connected with others despite all the noise.

Core Practice: Pay attention to people

You can use the practice of present-moment, non-judgmental awareness to direct your attention to other people. The following experiments will give you a sense of how you might do that. In the first experiment, you'll spend a few moments bringing an individual person to mind in as stable a way as you can. In the second experiment, you'll observe a meeting with curiosity rather than a busy and tribal mind. The third experiment asks you to do a simple visualization to reflect on connectedness.

Experiment: Notice a Person

Call an individual person to mind. Don't be too selective; just let that person's image appear in your awareness. For 30 seconds, make them the object of your attention. Just notice your experience of them, right here and right now. Whatever your relationship with them, pay attention to what arises in the present moment, without desire, and without aversion. If you get distracted, gently bring your attention back to the person without judgments.

When you're confronted with another person's image in your mind, your attention quickly becomes unstable! All the complications of interpersonal dynamics—informed by past experiences and thoughts of the future—immediately show up, pulling you away from noticing that person in the present moment. The practice is to notice the distraction, let it go, and bring your attention back to the person you have in mind.

Experiment: Be a Meeting Anthropologist

The next time you're in a meeting or at an event for your organization, observe behavior, body language, speech and attitudes as though you were an anthropologist. Imagine yourself with your field notebook, your binoculars, your professional interest in recording what you are witnessing. When you get pulled into thoughts of belonging and non-belonging, memories or predictions of people and your relationships with them, just let them go and come back to your core practice of stable attention.

An image of connectedness: the ocean

Here's a thought experiment to try, that explores the experience of paying attention to others from a metaphorical point of view.

Experiment: The Ocean

Imagine yourself as a wave in the ocean. You rise and fall, sometimes breaking into foam. You are aware of many other waves all around you. Though you are aware of yourself as an individual wave, you also know you are made of water, the same water that creates the other waves. In fact, there is no difference between you and them—only a different form that is quite temporary and fluid. As you continue to notice the waves on the ocean, gradually transform them in your mind's eye into a group of people. It could be a workgroup, or the people on a bus or train, or even a large crowd in a sports stadium. As you notice them, be aware that—whatever your differences—you are connected by your shared humanity, by your biology, by your home on this planet. Without needing to change anything, notice that connectedness.

The micropractices in the list below give you specific contexts for developing connectedness. Each practice has its own flavor, but the fundamental process—paying attention—remains the same.

STEP FIVE: BUILD THE HABIT

Cultivating the habit of connectedness

Growing a greater sense of connectedness between yourself, your team, and your larger organization is a matter of building new habits. Choose one or more of these micropractices and do it every day. See page 17 for more about building habits.

Connectedness Micropractices

Pay Attention to Your Humanity, page 164

Expand Your Circle of Concern, page 166

Pay Attention to the Other Point of View, page 169

Pay Attention to Your Perceptions of Others, page 171

What to expect as you build the habit

The practice of Connectedness works with a built-in cognitive apparatus that makes social interactions exceedingly complex and challenging. The practice of noticing other people does not make that apparatus go away. You're likely to see some fitful improvements in your ability to connect clearly with others, and there will be a certain amount of backsliding. But even improving your ability to notice the times and places when awareness is harder to come by is a major accomplishment. When a ship's captain makes a one-degree course correction, it doesn't take many miles for the ship's destination to be radically altered. Just keep at it, one person, one interaction, one meeting at a time. Be sure to acknowledge your successes, those times when you can see people clearly as they are and aren't consumed by your own thoughts and expectations. If you have a bad day or a bad interaction, let it go without judging yourself and try again. Building the muscle of connectedness takes time, and it's an ongoing process.

The Incident (continued)

A couple of weeks after the Ceres Project team resumes its meetings, the group has settled into an uneasy calm. The euphoria of the incident weekend has worn off, and the old tensions between the customer success team and the development team have started to bubble up again.

The upcoming team lunch is making Terra nervous. "What if it turns into a food fight?"

But the lunch goes better than Terra expected. George and Li Hua discover they have more in common than they thought, and although it was a challenge to convince Padma to step away from her meetings and join, everyone is glad she did—it turns out she has a lively sense of humor no-one had seen before. Terra is pleased and hopeful. "Sometimes just sharing a meal together does a world of good—it keeps us more human. We need to do that more often." (Micropractice: Pay Attention to Your Humanity)

Terra comes into the office the next day to find that she's been cc'd on an email from George to Li Hua. A new problem has cropped up with Ceres, and the note is full of grievance and aggression. There are exclamation points and a few too many words in all caps. "That George," Terra thinks. "Always defending his staff. It's like they can never do anything wrong. That whole group can be so demanding! I know Li Hua is going to freak out when she reads this. It'll be just another reason for her and her team to see themselves as victims."

Terra leans back in her chair. Takes a breath. And then she has a realization. She's not just witnessing tribal behavior: she's acting pretty tribal herself. Sometimes she sees George, Li Hua, and Padma as her adversaries rather than her allies. "Hmm. I probably can't expect the team to rally together if I'm also part of the problem." Sitting in her car the next morning, doing her two minutes of breathing, she remembers an empathy-building exercise she learned in her mindfulness class. "It's odd to visualize George as safe and happy. But why wouldn't I want

*that for him—especially if it helps the team? I'll give it a go."
(Micropractice: Expand your Circle of Concern)*

*A little practice seems to make a big difference. She begins to read the
steady stream of emails between George and Li Hua and their two teams
(which, unfortunately, seem be getting progressively more hostile) in a
different way. She's spending less time looking at what makes the two
groups wrong or difficult. She notices she's less likely to feel alienated
when George goes off on a rant, or feel frustrated with Li Hua and her
inclination to hide out, or with Padma and her tendency to be
overbooked. Terra is able to see them more clearly as they are, rather
than hoping they will somehow change their personalities. As a result,
Terra is more able to hear what they are saying, ask better questions,
and respond more thoughtfully.*

*Still, the friction between the customer service and development teams
continues to get worse. And it's not just confined to email anymore;
several meetings have ended in a tense silence rather than the discussion
the team needed. "I can be as nice and understanding as I want, but
that's not addressing the disconnects in the group. We need to find a
way to break down these barriers when we're talking about issues—not
just when we're bonding over lunch."*

*She asks for a meeting with Padma. "Not the easiest person to raise this
idea with," she thinks. But doing her best to stay focused, Terra pushes
ahead. "Padma, I've been thinking about the database corruption issue.
The way things are going on the team I worry we're going to have
something like that happen again before long. The bottom line is that we
need George and Li Hua—and their teams—to understand each other*

better. That session we did before we launched really helped. Can we bring everyone together again for a session to work on how we can all get along better? I have some ideas about that." Padma doesn't look up and keeps right on typing. "I knew it—this not an area Padma is very comfortable with," Terra thinks.

But Padma surprises her: "I agree with you," she says, and looks up. "I can't say too much about what's coming, but we do need the team to be working together now more than ever. Go ahead and schedule a couple of hours for the team to get together. I'll join you too."

Terra is pleased, relieved…but also a bit anxious. She knows the stakes for this workshop are a little higher. "We're so used to disregarding each other. This should be interesting." As the group files into the conference room, she's nervous but well prepared. She begins by laying out what she has noticed about the team's tendency to split into tribal factions. It's hard for them to disagree about the negative consequences. She reminds them how helpful the team lunch was, and how she hopes they'll keep up those social interactions. She goes on to share with them what she's been doing on her own to counterbalance her own tribal tendencies. Then she proposes they work together on two exercises to increase their connectedness: one to improve their ability to imagine the world from another person's point of view (Micropractice: Pay Attention to the Other Point of View), and one to improve their ability to validate what they imagine (Micropractice: Pay Attention to Your Perceptions of Others). "After all," she tells the group, "who knows what new storm is coming? Let's be prepared to face it together."

STEP SIX: KEEP IT RELEVANT

Agile and Scrum

When your team and your organization can build connectedness by applying sustained attention to each other as people, team members will collaborate more effectively and be less prone to the toxic effects of organizational factions (including departmental silos and tribal subgroups within teams). Team connectedness is a key assumption in the practice of Agile and Scrum software development. Agile and Scrum are perfect examples of how the power of connectedness can build effective teams that deliver great results in the face of great challenges.

Connected Agile

Agile software development includes a wide range of practices. The common characteristic of these practices is an incremental and iterative approach: do the work rapidly and in small batches, get feedback early and often, and repeat. At its founding in 2001, the Agile movement tied together many existing methodologies, and it has had a profound influence on many more methodologies since then. But at the heart of Agile is the concept of connectedness. The first phrase of the Agile Manifesto, the document that defined and continues to shape Agile work in all its flavors, is "Individuals and interactions over processes and tools."[28] A bit later the Manifesto raises the importance of connectedness still further: "Customer collaboration over contract negotiation." These are simple words, but powerful in their implications. Your relationships with the people you work with—and the people you are doing the work for—are more important to successful software development than how you do the work. In short: connectedness matters.

The abstract principles of the Manifesto are borne out in the day-to-day of technology delivery. Incremental and iterative development emerged in response to the need for results that are fast, responsive, and flexible (it's not called "Agile" for nothing). In the chaos and swirl of a complex delivery project that's constantly changing, it is ridiculously easy to get out of synch with the teammate in the cube next to you, let alone a customer on the other side of the planet. As the Manifesto suggests, all the processes and communication tools in the world can't outperform a healthy habit of human connectedness.

As Agile has matured, it has helped spawn a number of important movements. Two of the most widely used and critical are SAFe (Scaled Agile Framework) and DevOps. SAFe, as the name suggests, takes the concepts of Agile into large enterprise contexts. Heavy-duty processes to coordinate extended teams with hundreds of members loom large in SAFe. If anything, the greater complexity and potential for miscommunication on a large project makes developing the habit of connectedness in an explicit, deliberate way even more important. The DevOps movement (a term that mashes up "development" and "IT operations") emerged to expand the scope of close collaboration across organizational boundaries to include operations, information security, testing, architecture, data management, and more. Given the increased complexity and intensity of these interactions, there's all the more need for cultivating the habit of connectedness.

A practice for better Agile

All the Connectedness micropractices will create more connectedness within your team, and between your team and those you collaborate with. Anything you do to improve your ability to stay connected and overcome tribal boundaries will make you a better Agilist (or SAFe or DevOps practitioner). But there's one practice that may be especially helpful:

 Individually or as a team, use the micropractice Expand Your Circle of Concern. The simple act of bringing to mind — with an attitude of concern — those individuals and teams you work with elsewhere in the building, across the country or around the world will increase your connectedness. At the same time, it will improve the quality of your work and help you deliver better results.

There are many different ways to expand your circle of concern. From my base in Seattle I was working with a team in Calgary, Canada. I could see that my understanding of their world had its limits, and those limits were impacting the Agile development work we were doing together. So, I paid a visit. At it happened, I arrived during the week of the Calgary Stampede, a huge midsummer rodeo and festival that (as I thought) perfectly captured the spirit of the city. Thinking to build some solidarity, I went to the Stampede, watched some cattle roping, and bought a black cowboy hat. At lunch with the team the next day, I discovered I was the only owner of a cowboy hat at the table: for that group, the Stampede was not really the place to go. They had a good laugh at my expense—but my attempt to build a connection strengthened our relationship.

Connected Scrum

If the broader term "Agile" suggests coordination of work among multiple teams, "Scrum" zeroes in on the specifics of how individual teams work together.[29] The term comes from rugby, and it's a powerful image of a group working in close physical proximity, intently focused on doing a task together.

Three characteristics are foundational to an effective Scrum team: a clear set of role definitions, a healthy set of team ceremonies, and a commitment to Scrum values.

Connected but open: Paying attention to one another as people, building trust, and breaking down barriers—these are the key elements of Scrum team success. The two key roles on a Scrum team are product owner and Scrum master. Between the two they manage the vision of what the team needs to build, based on the organization's needs (that's the primary role of the product owner) and keep the team's own performance at a healthy level (the role of the Scrum master). But product owners and Scrum masters need to build the habit of connectedness with each other, with the team as a whole and with the larger organization.

Connected during ceremonies: At the heart of Scrum is a set of team "ceremonies": regular meetings where much of the work is done, including sprint planning, daily scrum (or standup), sprint review (or demo) and sprint retrospective. These activities, iterated every two to three weeks, create not just the work context but also the experience of connectedness for a Scrum team. Since the habitual nature of ceremonies has the potential to deaden them, the micropractice Pay Attention in Meetings explores ways to maintain stable and consistent attention during these ceremonies. But the effectiveness of team ceremonies is also dependent on the team's sense of connectedness. Here's why:

- If you're debating the level of effort for a particular work item in a *planning meeting,* connectedness will keep you from breaking into factions.
- At a *daily scrum* or *standup* meeting, connectedness will ensure you are fully aware of each other not just as resources for getting the job done, but also as human beings with lives outside the workplace.
- At a *sprint review* or *demo session* — particularly when stakeholders are present — connectedness will keep you from falling into defensive factions and enable open conversation.
- And in a *retrospective,* where anything from toxic argument to dead silence is possible, connectedness will help you say what needs to be said while preserving the health of your relationships. (Managing emotional reactivity plays a role as well. That's why we'll look more closely at a retrospective example in Chapter Four.)

Connected to the Scrum values: While Scrum is heavily focused on processes (and that's a good thing), the Scrum values of commitment, courage, focus, respect, and openness make it clear that Scrum is more than just a set of processes. Build the habit of connectedness and the Scrum values will come alive, helping any Scrum team thrive.

A practice for better Scrum

All the Connectedness micropractices will build the habit of connectedness to make your Scrum team stronger. To cultivate the Scrum values, try the following with your team:

 When the intensity rises, it's vital to use the micropractice Pay Attention to Your Humanity. The Scrum value of respect and commitment means more than just commitment to the work: it means commitment to each other.

My very first experience working with a Scrum team was in the role of product manager. I was the outside stakeholder that the product owner interfaced with. Since I was at a distance from the development team, I spend a lot of time on the phone with him and the Scrum master. It was a tense project with a lot of problems, but for the most part we maintained that vital sense of connectedness. One day, though, I hit my limit. "OK guys," I said, "there are some things I'm really frustrated about right now. Before we get into that, though I just want to tell you"—and I had to work very hard to say this in the moment…but I did—"I just want to tell you that my connection with you as human beings is much more important than however this project turns out." As I went on to lay out my concerns, it's not that the conversation was exactly easy, or happy. But we did manage to stay connected—to preserve the thread of our relationship—and that got us over the finish line faster and better than if the connection had been lost.

CHAPTER 3
Open-Mindedness

Relax your certainty and see with clarity.

Open-minded teams challenge assumptions, get as close to the facts as they can, and then act together based on shared understanding. To cultivate open-mindedness, stay aware of the inherent cognitive bias of the human thought-stream, and relate to that bias with humility and honesty.

STEP ONE: EMBRACE THE PARADOX

The paradox of thoughts beyond thinking

"Are unicorns extinct? Or just endangered?" On the *This American Life* episode "Kid Logic," Alex Blumberg relates several tales of people whose childhood beliefs survived into adulthood. These unexamined assumptions were only exploded when they inadvertently found their way into conversation (usually resulting in a long and embarrassed silence). Tooth fairies, a tissue box painted by trained monkeys, unicorns…these are just a few of the creative ideas humans can become attached to and hold with certainty for decades. In fact, all of us entertain unicorn thoughts—inconsistencies and logical fallacies we are unaware of.

The paradox of open-mindedness is that our brains are really good at thinking, but thinking can be full of inaccuracies that get us into big trouble. As long as you completely identify yourself with your thoughts, then you imagine your logic is air-tight, your arguments are unassailable, and your positions are irrefutable. Only by stepping away from identification with those thoughts can you begin to see the inevitable holes in your thinking.

In the story that follows, and in the rest of this chapter, you'll see this paradox at work. The way to improve your mental acuity is to suspend your thoughts for a moment and take a step back before thinking again.

STEP TWO: FIND YOUR MOTIVATION

Open-mindedness and your team

What causes some teams to maintain a clear and accurate view of circumstances, so they can make good decisions and address challenges effectively? Why do other teams seem to be perpetually out of touch with the reality of their situation , or stay snarled in constant disagreements? It has little to do with the relative intelligence of the teams or their leaders, and rarely has anything to do with how hard they work. Open-minded teams make better decisions and stay connected because they have the ability to **pay attention to the current circumstance as it is right here and right now,** not as they hope or fear it will be. In an atmosphere of healthy and collaborative discussion and debate, they freely acknowledge what's working well, challenge assumptions, and get as close to the truth as they can. These teams investigate the present moment, treating it like an endlessly fascinating research project. Will their current hypothesis prove to be correct, or will it need serious modification? They don't know yet, but they are interested in finding out.

In short, an aligned team has **the habit of open-mindedness**.

What is the quality of the decisions your team makes? What would be the impact of improving your ability to think and decide together?

The Initiative Kickoff

"Can we really be over the hump?" Terra wonders as she sits in her driveway one morning before beginning her daily breathing practice. For the first time in months she hadn't felt compelled to check her email before breakfast to see if some disaster had happened overnight. As the Ceres Project launch reaches its three-month milestone, things have settled down quite a bit. With the team working together in a more connected way, the backlog of issues has been reduced. Li Hua's team of developers and George's customer success team are working together on a new round of functionality, with a better shared understanding of each other and of the work. Sponsoring executive Padma is making an effort to stay engaged with the latest set of activities—and with the people working on them—despite juggling multiple priorities. The Ceres cross-functional team is meeting regularly, and both the tone and the effectiveness of the conversation have improved dramatically.

By the time Terra gets to the office, everything has changed. In her inbox is an all-hands email from Carlos, the CIO, announcing a major technology partnership with an artificial intelligence company. One of the bullet points on the long list of expected changes is a new AI technology that will "radically change the way customer service is delivered." According to the announcement, "in less than six months" the customer success team's processes will be "brand new and innovative" with "far lower staff costs," and the development team will be spending 100% of their time working in a "groundbreaking new technology platform."

Later that day, at the Ceres Project cross-functional team meeting, George leads off. "After all my customer success team has done for this company," he says, "this is how they treat us? It's so typical. I'm going to tell my people to start brushing up their resumes." Li Hua says, "I've spent the last three hours reading about this new partner's technology stack. I'm sending my whole team for a two-week training session on their environment." Padma turns to Terra. "Let's plan now to get this done in three months, so we have enough time to launch worldwide and avoid any risk of being late. I'm sure we can do that."

Terra, feeling a little sick, after mumbling a vague promise about starting the planning process tomorrow, manages to get the team back to the agenda. But she can't help noticing how everyone on the team has raced ahead to their own conclusions. George has assumed the worst for his team before he has fully understood what's coming and what the impact will be. Li Hua has jumped to the conclusion that she knows what the technical solution will be for her team. Padma has put a stake in the ground about planning before knowing anything about what specifically the work will consist of. Terra knows everyone is looking to her to make all these pieces fit together. "Well," she thinks as she walks out of the room, "I sure hope everyone will calm down in the next day or two."

Two months later, nothing is calmer. Juggling Ceres Project work and the implications of the new AI partnership has been as stressful as anything Terra has done. But after much frantic effort and a fair amount of wasted time, the picture has started to get clearer. The future of George's customer success team is not as dire as first anticipated. Though big changes are definitely coming, it turns out staffing levels won't actually change all that much. Sadly, George has lost some key people due to the uncertainty. Most of what Li Hua's development team needs to work on will build directly on what they've done before, and the expensive training wasn't really relevant. And unfortunately for Padma's reputation with the executive team, her vision of a three-month timeframe for the integration is now looking like eight months, based on the planning that Terra (working overtime) has led for the past several weeks.

Terra remains concerned about the team's ability to deliver and is a bit annoyed they weren't able to apply more effective thinking to the challenges they face. "We all made a bunch of assumptions and started running in all directions at once," she thinks. "It's really too bad!" She shakes her head, thinking of the staff departures, wasted training expenses, and unrealistic schedule expectations that could have been avoided. "I'm glad we finally have a clearer understanding of reality," she thinks. "But why did we waste weeks in unproductive chaos when we could have thought more accurately in the first place? There must be a better way to think!"

She and her data analyst friend Alice go for a long walk in the park. Despite all the hard work and frustration, Terra is surprisingly energized, and Alice has a little trouble keeping up with Terra's pace. "My team's habit of jumping to conclusions without good information is killing us," Terra tells Alice as they round the pond. "But if we can get more attentive and more connected, I'm sure we can learn to make better decisions. I just wish I knew how." "Sounds like cognitive bias to me," Alice says. "I have to watch out for that every day or my analysis turns into pure fantasy." "Really?" says Terra. "Tell me more."

STEP THREE: UNDERSTAND THE OBSTACLES

The biased brain

The human brain is a messy organic entity. Developed in environments very different from how we live today, it has complicated layers inherited from our common heritage with all forms of life. The prefrontal cortex—the rational, reasoning crown jewel of planetary intelligence, as it likes to think of itself— is full of assumptions about what's going on out there.

Those assumptions are based on precious little actual information. As neuroscientist and psychologist Lisa Feldman Barrett explains:

> *Like those ancient, mummified Egyptian pharaohs, the brain spends eternity entombed in a dark, silent box. It cannot get out and enjoy the world's marvels directly; it learns what is going on in the world only indirectly via scraps of information from the light, vibrations, and chemicals that become sights, sounds, smells, and so on. Your brain must figure out the meaning of those flashes and vibrations, and its main clues are your past experiences, which it constructs as simulations within its vast network of neural connections.*[30]

Hallucinations—that's how neuroscientist Anil Seth refers to the way the brain constructs experience from a limited flow of information.[31] "Hallucinations" seems like a dramatic term, but consider this: your brain operates in almost precisely the same way whether you are awake or dreaming. The only difference is that your awake brain gets a modest amount of external perceptual input. Consider that only 10% of the brain connections to your visual cortex are communicating input from the eyes to the rest of the brain. The other 90% of the connections are busy telling the visual cortex what it *should* see: making predictions.[32] This is why only one of three college students walking across the quad notice a clown riding on a unicycle.[33] Whether you're a college student or a CEO, what you see (and hear, and otherwise seem to perceive about the "world out there") is mostly predictions, with occasional confirmations from the outside world. A baseball player doesn't ever "see" a fastball coming at 100 miles per hour. The brain makes a prediction, and when the prediction is accurate the ballplayer hits a home run.

Much of the time those assumptions are perfectly adequate to handle the challenges of day to day life. For survival activities like crossing the savannah, finding food, or avoiding the spears thrown by a hostile tribe, our ancestors' brain predictions were very effective. And that's just as true for most of what we do in the contemporary world. But when humans encounter complexity, the predicting brain starts to run into problems.

Optical illusions are a great way to illustrate this predictive activity at work. Consider the "checker shadow illusion".[34] In the image on the left below, your brain insists on seeing A and B as different. But as you can see from the bar connecting A and B in the image on the right, they are in fact the same shade of grey.

There are multiple brain short-cuts at work here: first, the brain is making sense of the checkerboard pattern by slightly tweaking the perceived shade of gray depending on whether its context is a light square or a dark square. Secondly, to make sense of the relationship between objects in space, the brain interprets the visual data to support its theory that the cylinder is casting a shadow from a source of light on the right.

This same basic phenomenon is at work in a variety of ways at every level of cognition. When you see someone's expression, or hear a tone of voice, or read a text or email, you're making judgments based on predictions. An email titled "Important News" takes you into hope or skepticism or anxiety based on who it's from and whether a layoff is in the offing. Just as in the checkerboard illusion, you're predicting where the shadow lies.

Whether you manage projects with dozens of people or refactor a complex code base or prepare for a board presentation, you're still predicting. Every decision you make is based on predictions, and those predictions are inevitably based in turn on a small subset of real-world information.

When you factor in additional complicating factors like your personal psychology and character, your expectations, your current level of stress, your various types of reactivity, and the web of relationships you are embedded in, it is no wonder that you often make decisions based on inaccurate predictions.

Cognitive biases are consistently inaccurate predictions the brain makes in its attempt to interpret reality. The Wikipedia article "List of Cognitive Biases" includes 190 (and counting!) different decision-making, social, and memory errors,[35] and it seems that the more we learn about how the brain works, the more biases we discover.[36]

While there are dozens of biases to choose from, there are three that have particular impact on team alignment:

- **Negativity bias**, which inclines us to see reality as worse than it actually is, results from jumping to conclusions based on overly negative presuppositions.
- **Wishful thinking,** which inclines us to see reality as better than it actually is, also results from jumping to conclusions — but in this case based on overly positive presuppositions.

- **Confirmation bias** inclines us to perceive only what supports our existing views and beliefs.

Negativity bias

From the standpoint of survival, the rush to judgment makes sense. Consider the origins of negativity bias: say you're walking down the path through the savannah to your cave. It's a little later than you thought (due to a longer than usual nap). You can see by the shadows that the sun is going down, and you know it's getting to be saber-tooth tiger time. You're walking through some bushes, aware that a saber-tooth tiger might be lurking behind one of them. You proceed with caution, peering intently into the brush, checking for very long teeth. "No teeth, no teeth, no teeth; good, I can head home." Because you were tuned to problems, and looking for problems, you were able to avoid the problems and stay alive for another day.

In the modern conference room there are no saber-tooth tigers, but the brain's habit of looking for problems and threats is intact. Especially when people are under stress, it's almost inevitable they will focus on the negative, and thereby perceive reality as worse than it actually is. This can pull teams out of alignment in two ways. Sometimes a team collectively turns the worst case into the actual case. It resorts to desperate shortcuts, sinks into enervating despair, or retreats from creatively engaging problems. Other teams turn negativity on each other, focusing on all the reasons this person or that person isn't doing their job properly.

Wishful thinking

Rather than seeing the world as it appears to be based the best evidence you can find, wishful thinking sees the world as you would like it to be. The evolutionary and cognitive causes of the wishful thinking bias are not at all clear. It's not easy to say why the brain would have a mechanism that would bias us in favor of imagining a rosier-than-reality outcome.

One possible theory is that wishful thinking is a form of self-deception that humans use to convince themselves to believe something they wouldn't otherwise accept. Knowing how easily we can be spotted telling lies, we lie to ourselves first, so we'll have an easier time convincing others. According to this theory, we use wishful thinking to build social cohesion, specifically so we can persuade others to believe something we don't quite believe ourselves.[37]

Wishful thinking can indeed build team cohesion and esprit de corps—but it comes at a terrible price. A team engaged in wishful thinking isn't pulled out of alignment during the lollipops-and-rainbows phase, but during the wake-up-and-smell-the-coffee phase. If they are based on wishful thinking rather than a careful consideration of reality, all the trust and goodwill that was generated during the rousing kickoff meeting or company retreat backfires into delays, frustration, and failure (compounded of course by negativity bias). How many times have you looked back at the smoking wreckage that resulted in the wake of wishful thinking (by you and others) and said, "We should have

known better?" You probably did, but convinced yourself
otherwise.

Whether it's a survival-based jump to a negative conclusion or a
social-cohesion-based rush to a positive one, negativity bias and
wishful thinking take you away from accurately evaluating the
true nature of the circumstances you're addressing, and pull you
and your team out of alignment with each other and with your
purpose.

Confirmation bias

> Be careful. People like to be told what they already
> know….What people think they want is news, but
> what they really crave is olds…Not news but olds,
> telling people that what they think they already
> know is true.

As Terry Pratchett points out in the quote above, from his novel
The Truth: A Novel of Discworld, confirmation bias is part of our
everyday cognitive apparatus. The most evident example today is
in the political world, where partisan content provided by media
outlets is consumed almost entirely by people who already share
those views. We don't seek information, we seek confirmation of
what we believe. That's just as true when you're looking at
project data as when you're reading the news.

Filtering information has an important survival benefit: our
ancestors needed to be able to disregard the gentle swaying of the
tall grass in the breeze and spot the movement of the saber-tooth

tiger behind it. We need filters just as much today to function in a highly complex, information-overloaded day-to-day world.

But the filtering effect of confirmation bias makes it harder for teams to stay aligned with each other and with their goals. The filters you apply skew your interpretation of what's actually happening and what needs to happen. Not only does this make it harder to keep the team moving effectively in the same direction, it also amplifies the effects of negativity bias and wishful thinking, since confirmation bias makes it easy to find data that supports your gloomy (or rosy) outlook.

STEP FOUR: UNDERSTAND THE CORE PRACTICE

Pay attention to your judgments

Biased thinking is fundamental to the way your brain operates, so deliberately rooting out even one bias, if it's possible at all, would be fiendishly difficult. Mastering the three biases we've discussed, let alone the entire list of 190+, is beyond hope. So, what can you do instead?

Chapter One introduced the habit of stable attention, developed by practicing present-moment, non-judgmental awareness. If inaccurate judgment is the primary characteristic of cognitive bias, the faculty of non-judgmental present-moment awareness is the remedy. Use non-judgmental awareness to examine your thought-stream. It will help you work with cognitive bias in a fruitful and sustained way.

Two caveats about non-judgmental awareness

The phrase "non-judgmental awareness" requires two very important caveats. First, "non-judgmental" does not prevent you from making decisions. And second, some of the most important judgments you make are the ones you're not aware of.

Discernment and decision

The purpose of suspending judgment is to see as accurately as possible what is actually going on: applying *discernment*. With discernment your intent is to see what is really so, rather than jumping to conclusions of good or bad, desirable or undesirable, suitable or unsuitable. Discernment enables you to *make a decision* in a deliberate way, based on the best information you have.

Implicit bias

You might apply non-judgmental awareness to a situation, and still be led astray by judgments you weren't aware of. That's because many of our biases are completely unknown to us (this is called **implicit bias**). This may be the most difficult of all the nasty realities of cognitive bias. Implicit bias is held in the unconscious mind, and so (as the Kirwan Institute at Ohio State describes it) "implicit biases are not accessible through introspection."[38] In other words, we can't see our implicit biases—only their effects.

Implicit bias is a deep social and moral issue worthy of attention and remediation. The immediate remedy is to apply non-judgmental awareness not just *before* discernment, but also *after*. Decisions have a way of closing down our openness, and so sustained curiosity is most important after a decision, so that you can stay open to becoming aware of assumptions that are operating unconsciously.

Core Practice: Pay attention to your bias

The practice of present-moment, non-judgmental awareness directed at your own assumptions or judgments can help you identify much of your bias. To address implicit bias (biases you are not consciously aware of), couple this practice with a willingness to seek feedback about your thinking from others.

The following is a series of experiments you can use to notice how cognitive bias is at work in your everyday thinking. These exercises involve a little writing—that's a useful way to focus your attention on your own thought processes (which tend to be especially wiggly and unstable). As I've found sitting through many a boring lecture, taking notes helps you pay attention! Even so, your mind is still likely to wander. As with our earlier experiments, if that happens, just notice it, let it go, and return to the task at hand.

Experiment: Expecting the Worst

Consider a circumstance when you assumed the worst and things turned out better than expected. For example: a change in your workplace, a social event, a predicted snowstorm that never happened. Spend a few minutes to make a list of the thought processes that led you to predict a negative outcome. Without making judgments of yourself, and staying with the memory, just notice the nature of your thinking at that time. What were your assumptions? What memories and expectations did you draw on? What logical leaps did you make?

The aim of this exercise, and the next one, is to notice your own thinking and decisions, not those of other people. As much as you can, stay focused on your recollection of the workings of your own mind.

Experiment: Hoping for the Best

Recall a time when wishful thinking led you to hope for a better-than-realistic outcome. This might have been a work project or something from your personal life. Take a few minutes to create a list of the kinds of thinking that led you to predict a better outcome than was likely. What led you to miss the warning signs? Did social costs distract you from seeing the situation more clearly? Would there have been emotional costs? How might you have thought and acted differently to avoid wishful thinking?

An image of open-mindedness: a clear blue sky

The fundamental quality of non-judgmental awareness is a sense of space around those moments when you are inclined to rush to judgment. That space can reduce stress and create an experience of relaxation. Space allows you to pause for reflection before jumping to a conclusion. Space replaces a hunger for closure with a hunger for understanding, and lets you stay open even after you've made a decision. Here's an image you might experiment with, to disentangle yourself from your thoughts and view them with clarity.

Experiment: The Clear Blue Sky

Imagine a clear blue cloudless sky. The sun is shining, and you might feel a gentle breeze or hear birds singing—but the main thing you notice is the vast, open, endless sky. After a few seconds, notice a small, white, fluffy cloud floating by. It's one of your thoughts. But it's surrounded by that expansive space of sky. The cloud may dissolve and reform, changing its shape. But you remain open, noticing the sky and the passing clouds with patient, aware, stable attention. Stay with the image for 30 seconds or so.

An ally: curiosity

One fundamental characteristic of non-judgmental awareness is curiosity, our built-in appetite for information and understanding. Psychologically, curiosity has much in common with hunger. It's a hunger for understanding.[39] Curiosity fuels the desire to learn, and to lean in to the unknown. It's a healthy appetite, leading to questions like, "What about this situation don't I understand? Can I discover something new?" A curious, open mindset can transform the anxiety of uncertainty into an occasion for enjoyment and even adventure.

Experiment: Curiosity

Imagine yourself on a path through a forest. You're lost in thought, puzzling out a problem (it might be work-related). Then you spot a sign: "Scenic Overlook," with an arrow pointing to a side path that winds off through the trees. Curious? You direct your steps onto the side path, scanning ahead through the underbrush as you negotiate the twists and turns. Ahead there's a parting of the trees, and the hint of a blue vista beyond. Can you feel your excitement growing? Your hunger to experience whatever view lies ahead? Tune in to that sensation of curiosity and wonder. Another 30 seconds, a few more steps, and the trees fall away, and you step out onto an enormous exposed boulder overlooking a canyon. Notice the sensation of wonder and satisfaction as your busy thoughts fall away and you drink in all there is to experience in this landscape. Somehow, this is the perfect new context for thinking about your problem. For now, you're just enjoying the view.

The micropractices listed below provide a few starting points for developing open-mindedness. Each practice focuses on a different context, but the core activity of paying closer attention to your thoughts, and especially your judgments, is the same.

STEP FIVE: BUILD THE HABIT

Cultivating the habit of open-mindedness

You and your team can develop a greater capacity for open-mindedness. Choose one or more of these micropractices and do it every day. See page 17 for more about building habits.

Open-Mindedness Micropractices

Pay Attention to the Good, page 174

Pay Attention to the Planning Fallacy, page 178

Pay Attention to Honesty and Humility, page 181

Pay Attention to Your Team's Wisdom, page 184

What to expect as you build the habit

Cognitive bias is a natural part of being human. In seeking to mitigate the effects of biases on team alignment, the goal (as with all the remedies in this book) is not to change your humanity, but to cultivate your capacity for greater awareness in order to manage your biases. In short, this means becoming more consistently aware of your tendency to make unfounded judgments.

You'll fall back into the habit of acting unconsciously out of your biases in a heartbeat. When that happens, just notice it, let it go, and continue the practice. Becoming aware of your biases is cause for celebration—that means you're becoming less victimized by them. It's the perfect opportunity to notice how your remarkable brain works—so beautiful, and so flawed! As you work on building micropractices into habits, what you'll notice is not an elimination of biases but rather a growing awareness of them, and a greater ability to account for them when you make decisions or take actions.

The Initiative Kickoff (continued)

"Just six months to go." Terra wakes up with a start and realizes that what she was dreaming is actually true. She really does have another six months of AI integration intensity ahead of her. The team has put some process improvements in place during the last two months, and the

changes have been valuable: communications are improved, turnaround times are faster, and handoffs from one team to another are cleaner. But there's still plenty of reason to be concerned. Driving in to the office, Terra wonders, "The processes are better, but are we really thinking better?"

On the way to work that morning, she reflects on yesterday's walkthrough of some new business process workflows. George and his team had worked hard on these flows and were clearly proud of what they had done—though George acknowledged that they had a long way to go. Surprisingly, Li Hua was critical of the workflows, saying that they were too high-level and didn't account for enough exceptional cases. Terra is glad that Li Hua was willing to speak up, but her comments did create a problem. George's team made a lot of progress, laying down a solid foundation for what lies ahead—and yet the team had spent the whole meeting talking about potential problems. When Terra thinks back to earlier meetings, she can see where Li Hua picked up the habit of criticism. Both George and Padma regularly deconstruct the good work others have done (including Li Hua). "It's as though we all think our only job is to find flaws," Terra thinks. "But that doesn't really get us closer to the truth. Not only is that creating a lot of tension, I think it's slowing us down. We're disregarding some good work that's being done. And sometimes we can end up building much more functionality than we actually need."

As she pulls into the company's parking lot, Terra sees Alice's Kia and remembers their conversation in the park. "This negativity is one of the cognitive biases Alice was talking about. Next time someone on the team presents something they worked hard on, I want to make sure we all acknowledge it. Of course we'll then proceed to critique. But I bet the critique will be more useful (and better received!) if it's in the context of appreciation. I actually don't think it will be that hard to do." The next day, she takes Li Hua and George to lunch and shares a few suggestions with them. They agree to try some changes—not just to the cross-functional team meetings, but also to the way they work with their own teams. (Micropractice: Pay Attention to the Good)

At first the cross-functional team finds the practice of acknowledging successes with appreciation a bit uncomfortable ("We're going to lose our edge!" one person complains). But what feels awkward at first starts to become natural, and both morale and the quality and speed of the work begin to tick up. When Li Hua thinks she sees a flaw in George's logic, rather than attacking she starts by saying, "I want to make sure I understand you—I can see you've put a lot of thought into this." Even George has been caught muttering a "thank you" at the end of a demo. As both George and Li Hua relax, the discussions about missing pieces or wrong assumptions get clearer and more open—and in fact, are surfacing real problems that would have been missed back in the tense "all-critique" days.

Meanwhile, Terra is having some issues with Padma and Carlos. At her meetings with the two of them, Carlos is continually asking what can be done to shorten up the schedule. "I don't really see why this work should be taking so long," Carlos frequently says. "Didn't we invest in a bunch of process improvements?" The more Terra tries to unpack the details of the work, the more he wants to collapse them together into vague bundles that can be "trimmed down" to save weeks of work.

To Terra's surprise, Padma is the one who challenges Carlos: "We all feel under the gun here—you more than anyone. But just because we want the project to take less time, that doesn't mean it will." Terra sees an opportunity. "Can I make a suggestion?" Carlos and Padma swivel to look at her. "Have you ever heard of the 'planning fallacy'?" (Micropractice: Pay Attention to the Planning Fallacy)

Over the next several meetings the conversations with Carlos and Padma become more productive and realistic. Carlos isn't happy with the schedule (since his CEO and the board are not happy with the schedule) but he understands the reality and can defend it with conviction.

With three months to go, the intensity has ramped up, but so far teams and leaders are staying pretty well aligned "Now we just need to stay on course," Terra thinks. She is now much more aware of cognitive bias. When an estimate seems too optimistic, she challenges it. When an unexpected problem leads the team into catastrophic thinking, she challenges it. When she doesn't know the answer to a question, she says so. She starts to regularly ask the questions "what do we know is true?" and "what do we not know?" (Micropractice: Pay Attention to Honesty and Humility).

Two months before launch, there's a serious snag. The AI technology partner can't deliver a key piece of functionality that's crucial to the project. At least 30% of the business benefit evaporates overnight. After an all-night emergency board meeting, Carlos calls the team together first thing in the morning. "Sorry, everyone. I'm a little ragged this morning. But I wanted to let you know that we've decided to keep going with the project. It's still worthwhile to the company. But we need to make a lot of decisions in the next week. Everyone strap on your thinking caps—this is not going to be easy." He turns to Terra. "Why don't you and Padma meet me in my office? Let's talk about how we're going to facilitate this."

As Terra stops by the kitchen to make herself a cup of tea, she thinks, "Whatever happens, I'm going to do everything I can to make sure decisions are based on as much truth as possible—and to do that we need to hear everyone's voice." (Micropractice: Pay Attention to Your Team's Wisdom)

STEP SIX: KEEP IT RELEVANT

Strategic planning and innovation

In this section, let's consider how open-mindedness can be used in strategic planning and innovation, two processes that are crucially important at both the organizational and the team level.

Open-minded planning

Strategic planning is the process an organization uses to define its strategic direction and make decisions about how to allocate resources to achieve that end. Although it's commonly thought of as an organization-wide annual activity, strategic planning is at work every day in the life of a team. Regardless of the scope of planning work you need to do, it's essential to maintain a healthy sensitivity to cognitive bias, and a consistent practice of open-mindedness to mitigate its effects

This is true throughout the sweep of the planning process, from analysis to strategic decision making, to setting goals and measures, to the way you structure the work and define roles for people, to the ways you budget for, reward, and evaluate the work. While we could fruitfully look at the impact of cognitive bias on each of these stages, let's focus on one commonly used planning activity: the SWOT analysis.

A SWOT (Strengths/Weaknesses/Opportunities/Threats) analysis is a structured way for you and your team to evaluate your potential to accomplish a strategic objective. Key to the technique is the ability to accurately evaluate the favorable and unfavorable factors in your internal and external environment.

One of the beauties of the SWOT analysis is that it speaks in the language of survival: our ancestors on the savannah probably used a similar approach to determine whether they should make a run to the water hole before it gets dark. The concerns that a SWOT analysis addresses should be a clue that your ancestral biases are likely to play a heavy part in the thinking you do, even when you're in the safety of an air-conditioned office.

Let's consider each element of the analysis from a cognitive bias point of view. We'll be looking just at the three biases we focused on in this chapter—but be aware there are dozens more waiting to trip you up.

Strengths: How is negativity bias preventing you from seeing what is unique and powerful about your company, your team, or your own abilities? Is a perceived strength actually just wishful thinking? When you look carefully at your strengths—through data, or interviews with staff or customers—does confirmation bias driven by negativity or wishful thinking skew what you see?

Weaknesses: Weaknesses are particularly scary, so multiple biases crowd around. You may be obsessed by a weakness (the product of negativity bias) or in denial of it (a result of wishful thinking). Just like a sore tooth that gets all your attention, confirmation bias might cause you to feel that one of your weaknesses is the biggest thing in your world. Is that really true?

Opportunities: There's often a highly desirable outcome—a major potential revenue stream, customer segment, or strategic alliance—that your CEO is pushing for and everyone wants. Does the social pressure drive you into wishful thinking? Or do you find yourself managing your uncertainty or fear of failure by falling into negativity bias? Whichever way you go, you're likely to feel intense pressure to look for confirmation as you do your analysis.

Threats: The experience of threat activates your cognitive biases (perhaps more than anything else, threats are what caused cognitive biases to develop in the first place). Maybe that upstart competitor will just go away. Or maybe they'll become the next Uber. How can you make an evaluation with as much clarity as possible, not looking for what you hope or fear to see, but what is actually so?

The habit of open-mindedness won't make any of the challenges to creating a clean and accurate SWOT analysis go away. But by cultivating the habit, you'll ensure that questions like those above will stay in your awareness as you do your work.

A practice for better strategic planning

All the Open-Mindedness micropractices will help you create a better SWOT analysis and make every step of the strategic planning process yield more accurate and useful results. Here's one practice that is sure to make things better:

 At the beginning, middle, and end of your next SWOT analysis (or any strategic planning activity), use the Pay Attention to Honesty and Humility micropractice.

A story about opportunity and honesty: A senior executive at a software company I worked with was determined to expand a product offering internationally. Since I was responsible for the team that translated the software into other languages, I was involved in a lot of those conversations. At one meeting when he was insisting we add yet more languages to our list (without, of course, giving us any additional resources), I was reminded of the story about the monkey who put his hand in a cookie jar, grabbed a fistful of cookies, and then was unable to get his hand out of the jar. Not wanting to relinquish the prize, he kept tugging, and kept on being stuck. In the end, we did find a way to add the languages, the hoped-for revenue didn't come, and the executive moved on to champion another pet project.

In stark contrast to this was Ethelyn Simon, the founder of EKS Publishing, who gave me my start in the work world. I worked closely with Ethelyn for several years, helping her fulfill her vision of delivering high-quality Hebrew-language-learning materials to adult learners. Though she was not always the easiest person to work with, Ethelyn was relentlessly honest, and just about as humble as she was honest. At the end of the day, all she cared about was getting the best possible result. She was constantly instructing individuals using our materials and listening carefully to their feedback. Even when she hated hearing what these test students had to say, she listened, and she made her young and overly confident staff members listen, and we made changes. That's the mindset that can overcome cognitive bias and see a larger strategic landscape clearly. Ethelyn started her company nearly 40 years ago and the products she created are still among the best on the market.

Open-minded innovation

The ability to generate and implement creative solutions that didn't previously exist is one of the most important and challenging aspects of your work, regardless of your role (executive, team lead, or individual contributor) and your environment (startup or large organization).

Geoffrey Moore's *Crossing the Chasm*, Tom Kelley's *The Ten Faces of Innovation*, and Clayton M. Christensen's *The Innovator's Dilemma* are just three of the many approaches companies and individuals use to stimulate innovation. There are also many frameworks for supporting the creativity required for innovation, from IDEO's Design Thinking methodology to Michael Michalko's *ThinkerToys* to Julia Cameron's *The Artist's Way*.

There is one prerequisite for all these approaches. To make new connections we must overcome the power of habit, the conventional pathways of thinking that prevent us from seeing possibilities and incline us to fall back on pre-existing assumptions. We don't have to look very far to find one of the key contributors to habitual thinking: cognitive bias. When you're trying to think outside the box, cognitive bias puts you right back inside. If you're trying to imagine future possibilities and make new connections, you don't want to be hamstrung by negativity. You don't want to drift off into the vague pleasures of wishful thinking. And you don't want your confirmation bias to cause you to see only what you expect to see.

It's important to take positive action to stimulate your creativity. Solicit diverse points of view. Make unorthodox connections. Draw mind maps. Use creativity techniques like the Exquisite Corpse or automatic writing. But at the same time, don't forget to continue to work on building the habit of open-mindedness.

The following are some specific ways the cognitive biases discussed in this chapter inhibit creativity, and what you can do to minimize their impact:

Negativity bias: Creativity consultant Aaron Schmookler of The Yes Works says "Problem solving is hard. Keeping an open mind and challenging ourselves is taxing and costly. The dopamine hit we get when we take a step back to celebrate fuels our ability to keep facing the punishing hunt for more progress tomorrow." [40] While a focus on dangers and threats is at times essential for short-term survival, it is a tremendous inhibitor of creativity. Lean in to possibilities. Be eager to spot the good, and be determined to sink into the joy of each accomplishment. That's the way to open up creative possibilities all around you.

Wishful thinking: Creativity requires the free play of the mind. You need to make plenty of room for wildly imaginative associations in the pursuit of new possibilities. But wishful thinking is something else. It can inhibit creativity and innovation, by introducing the more or less passive hope that *imagination alone* will fix everything. Wishful thinking is satisfying, but it doesn't create. It stops short of the important element of actually bringing into being what you imagine. To stay clear of wishful thinking, make responsibility for action an integral part of your creative work.

Confirmation bias: This may be the ultimate creativity killer. If you only see what you expect to see, you will always be bounded by your own limitations. You can counteract the influence of confirmation bias by embarking on any innovation activity with a mindset of being willing to go where you haven't been before. Curiosity—a hunger to understand what isn't yet known—keeps this mindset alive when pressure, impatience, or fatigue are leading you back to the familiar. Slowing down also helps prevent the tendency to fall back into habit.

A practice for better innovation

The Open-Mindedness micropractices will strengthen your resistance to cognitive bias and improve your ability to innovate. Since being creative with other people is one sure way to minimize the effects of bias, team-oriented practices are particularly effective. Here's one to try:

 Fuel innovation by liberal use of celebration, using the micropractice Pay Attention to the Good.

When I consider all the launch parties and company celebrations I've been part of, the one that stands out is surprising. And yet it was powerfully effective in its context. I was working with a company that had a large pool of vendors from around the world that needed to enroll in a supplier program. We were building an online tool that would enable each new vendor to answer a series of questions to determine their level of tax withholding. The team I was leading worked long and hard to get the fussy details of the interface, the logic of the online interview workflow, and compliance with IRS requirements implemented correctly. When the interview launched, we were quite proud of what we had done. However, the results (a tax interview? really?) seemed too esoteric and boring to be of much interest to the rest of the company—most of our colleagues were working on much cooler and more innovative projects. Nevertheless, the team was determined to celebrate in a public way. So we threw a launch party, and invited our guests to fill out a paper-based simulated "tax interview." Each person who completed the interview received a bag of gold coin chocolates: their "refund." We were all astonished at the enthusiasm with which our co-workers flocked up to the interview table to fill out a (completely meaningless) paper form and get their candy. But it was also thrilling for all of us. It showed us that we had made a difference and had earned the right to share our pride with others. The energy from that party fueled the team toward a string of future successes addressing other vendor-finance-related challenges.

CHAPTER 4
Self-Awareness

Notice your body and encounter your mind.

The self-aware team acknowledges the emotional impact of adversity and stays resilient by addressing reactions to stress and change together. To cultivate self-awareness, pay attention to your reactivity and its influence on your thinking. In this way your team can bridge the gap between emotional experience and rational thought.

STEP ONE: EMBRACE THE PARADOX

The paradox of mind and body

In the film *The Adventures of Baron Munchausen*, Robin Williams appears as the King of the Moon. This monarch has the unusual capability of detaching his head ("where the brilliant and important parts are located") from the rest of his body. The head comments on their former relationship: "It is hard to believe my body and I were ever attached. We are so totally incompatible. I mean, he is still dangling from the food chain and I am in the stars…oh, it is so unmetaphysical!" Eventually, though, even the King of the Moon must be reluctantly reunited with his body.

It may be tempting to think, like the King of the Moon, that the purity of your thoughts and perceptions is untainted by your physicality. But the paradox of self-awareness is that you can never be fully aware of who you are unless you are able to pay attention to your body and what it is telling you. Though we might sometimes believe otherwise, it's often the united wisdom of mind and body—head and heart—that gives us the most unerring view of what is so. And even when the body's reactivity is an obstacle to your thinking (as is sometimes the case), you must acknowledge its participation, so you can find your way to clarity.

STEP TWO: FIND YOUR MOTIVATION

Self-awareness and your team

Why can some teams handle the emotion that comes with adversity in an open and productive way, while others remain rigid and in denial? Self-aware teams are interested in understanding every aspect of their experience, including their emotions. They recognize their work together requires them to **pay attention to their reactions right here and right now**. They know emotions, left unacknowledged, can be profoundly disruptive. So, although it's not always easy or comfortable, self-aware teams stay open to the whole range of emotional possibilities, from fear and anger to joy and sadness. Whatever emotions rise in the moment, they don't drive the team apart, but become an opportunity to bring the team together into more powerful alignment. Individually and as a team, they can respond productively to feelings—especially reactive feelings—by acknowledging and working through them and finding appropriate resolutions. No matter what challenges arise, the team sticks together, addressing the actual risk rather than amplifying the risk by letting reactions get the best of them.

In short, an aligned team has the habit of **self-awareness**.

How resilient to challenges and adversity is your team? What would be the impact of becoming more self-aware, individually and as a team, as you navigate the pressures of working together?

The Post-Mortem Meeting

"It's going to be OK," Terra tells herself as she walks into the conference room. Still, she can't help but feel disheartened. The AI project launched on time, and the team seemed to work great together. And yet, just two weeks after launch, there was another catastrophic database failure — just like last time. In the push to get the release out the door, George's customer success team had gotten backdoor access to the database over development manager Li Hua's objections — just like last time. Just like last time, bad data got into the system. And so, once again the team is about to have another tense post-mortem meeting.

The room is packed. There are three main groups in the meeting: application development VP Padma and several senior executives, including Carlos, the CIO. Li Hua together with her whole team of software and security engineers. George with his whole team of customer success staff. Terra is facilitating, but she knows it's not what she has to say that matters. With a mixture of anticipation and anxiety, she waits to hear what transpires.

After Terra's kickoff, Padma tries to set the tone. "Our goal here is to uncover what went wrong and how we can fix it. This is not about assigning blame." But Carlos subverts her message: "People, we can't let this happen again. I want to know what happened, and who's responsible. I want answers!" Seeing an opening, and in a fighting mood, George starts in: *"Let me read a few choice emails from angry customers. Some of them swear they'll never work with us again."*

As George reads, the tension grows. Li Hua, who thought she was prepared for a fight, finds herself frozen instead. She had planned to say, "We warned you that giving George access to the database was going to create problems. But we were told the project couldn't wait." But she doesn't say that, and instead sits in silence. In the increasing discomfort in the room, Padma is relieved to hear her phone buzz. It's an urgent text about another project. "So sorry, folks," she says as she heads out the door. "I'll follow up with you after the meeting." It's clear that she's happy to take the first opportunity to flee.

Terra does her best to keep the meeting on track, with limited success. Afterward, she reflects on all the anger expressed, all the things that needed to be said that were left unsaid, and the key participants who disappeared literally or virtually. None of the core issues were addressed, which means the team hasn't lowered the odds of a similar issue cropping up again. Unless something changes, Terra's pretty sure future post-mortem meetings will go exactly the same way. It's discouraging. "After all the work we've done together, everyone's gone right back to their reactions. Just like the last post-mortem," she thinks.

"Why are these post-mortem meetings always ruled by emotions...and yet we never talk about emotions?" she wonders. There must be a way to call attention to the reactions that are happening, so the team can move past them into a real discussion of the issues.

Terra's data analyst friend Alice takes her to lunch. "Emotional reactions," Terra says, as Alice takes a bite of burrito. "After all our progress and increased productivity, that's still a big problem. Where can I find some help with that?" Alice chews thoughtfully. "Wait a minute," Terra says, "Didn't you go through that lunchtime emotional intelligence workshop a couple of months ago? Was it any good?"

"I did," Alice says. "I do think a lot of that material could be useful for your team. But you need to find a way to apply it in context — that's the key to keeping it from being just another nice set of ideas."

STEP THREE: UNDERSTAND THE OBSTACLES

The reactive brain

There is a basic level of self-awareness teams can't afford to ignore: the way we each respond when we feel threatened. When challenges come, awareness of this threat response plays an important role in keeping a team aligned.

Fight, flee, freeze

Back in the ancestral savannahs of Africa, the survival algorithm was pretty simple. When the saber-toothed tiger showed up, you had three options. You could fight the tiger (if you had a spear or a big rock, and/or had a lot of buddies around). You could run from the tiger (which might work if it had a sore paw). You could freeze and hope the tiger wouldn't spot you.

As long as the tiger was around, there wasn't much time to think. Your brain was evaluating your options for action with great rapidity, making a quick decision to select the appropriate option for the circumstances. Whatever cave-painting or log-drumming ideas you may have been thinking about before the tiger showed up, they disappeared completely from your consciousness. Your mental process became totally focused on taking immediate action: fight, flee, or freeze. Your body quickly reacted, too: your heart beat faster to pump more blood, adrenaline flowed to get your muscles ready to move, and your eyes dilated so you could take in more visual information. It's only when the tiger wandered away that you could return to your normal mental and physical state (probably after a good stiff drink of fermented mammoth milk).

Tigers in the imagination

Today there are no tigers prowling the streets. If we humans were another kind of animal, we might relax and enjoy the predator-free environment (just watch a crow hopping casually across the street). But in the human mind with its powerful imagination, the tigers live on. When you get a nasty email or an audit notice, you sense the gleaming fangs of immediate threat, and you do what all animals do when they sense immediate threat: decide whether to fight, flee or freeze. Your mind goes on high alert, and the threat shows up in your body in very predictable ways too, since your body is gearing up to take action. Your heart rate goes up, your adrenaline flows, your eyes dilate—all the physical tools you need to deal with a physical threat.

The human capacity for metaphorical thinking—applying the experience from one context to a different context—means you experience visceral survival threats from events that do not threaten your survival. My heart has started pounding plenty of times when I received worrisome emails, even though none of them was literally lethal. Reactive fighting, fleeing, or freezing also appear in metaphorical ways. For example, you might become passive-aggressive. You might create emotional and social distance. You might shut down and deny your emotions entirely. Every muscle and organ in your body may be prepping you to hurl a rock at your foe, but the action you take is to bang out an angry email response. Your heart may be pounding and your breath more rapid to prime you to dash for the woods, but instead you stay up late updating the project plan or fixing bugs.

When the experience of threat dies away, your state of threat-induced arousal calms down and the world looks very different. Your thinking is normal, your body experience is normal, and it's hard to remember what you were so upset about. This shift in experience is one of the things that makes retrospectives of challenging projects so difficult.

Reactivity is sticky

Why do you read dozens of emails a day, and attend scores of meetings a month, but only experience a few of them as threatening your survival? Why does *that* co-worker, *that* executive, or *that* customer set off all the alarm bells? Why do you perceive threats in some circumstances but not in others? The answer lies in a specific brain structure and its ability to remember.

The brain territory primarily responsible for taking quick action in response to a threat is the amygdala, a pair of almond-shaped structures in the temporal nodes. Simply said, the amygdala and some related structures function as the **reactive brain**. The reactive brain has its own dedicated memory processing function – it specializes in remembering traumas. Whatever gets remembered by the reactive brain, stays in the reactive brain, unless you very deliberately and explicitly work to learn a different response.[41] You may not even be able to access that memory when you don't feel under threat—but as soon as you do, the memory comes right up again. This is very handy when the threat is literal and real (like the distinctive glint of saber-tooth tiger fangs in the moonlight). But when it comes to metaphorical threats (and most of the threats that impact team cohesiveness are metaphorical), amygdala-based memories of individual or team traumas can create a lot of confusion. The unexpected is like a sniper, damaging team effectiveness with hidden attacks no-one anticipated.

If you are a human being, throughout your life you have collected all sorts of traumas large and small. Like all humans, you have a catalog of pain and rejection—experiences of fear and anger and numbness—that constantly pop up to create outsized reactions. That's why much of your present reactivity, when it happens, has little to do with what's actually happening, and a lot to do with the past.

When you find yourself more angry, fearful or upset than you might reasonably suppose you would be, it's likely you're experiencing a trigger: a current experience that you associate with a past experience, which then initiates the built-up reactivity response. And there you are, fighting or fleeing or freezing in all sorts of creative and displaced ways, ways that have little or nothing to do with the current situation. It can be very counterproductive to getting the work done. Having an awareness of those triggering experiences, and being able to separate what's happening now from what happened then, is a key self-awareness skill. That skill has to be developed in the rational brain, though, and not just in the reactive brain. Because when you're reacting...you're busy reacting.

Constructing emotions

With such a direct connection between your bodily reaction and your emotional experience, and such well-developed reactivity processes, why do emotions seem so mysterious and uncontrollable? The reason lies in the difference between all the systems we've been talking about and your language-oriented reasoning. Your reactivity apparatus is non-linguistic, communicating to you through feelings and sensations, and stirring you to response with an urgency that doesn't wait around for the niceties of cogitation and definition. And the rational parts of your brain, particularly the prefrontal cortex, which prefers to make sense of the world in ways that are clear, coherent, and linguistically articulate, isn't happy with the nature and quality of the inarticulate, feeling-oriented information it's getting. Simply put, there's a gap between your emotions and your reason.

A useful explanation of this gap is offered by Lisa Feldman Barrett in her book *How Emotions Are Made*.[42] Barrett delineates the apparatus I've described above, and then goes on to talk about the linguistic component of emotion. Self-awareness is, in part, the ability to describe those non-linguistic feelings with accuracy. If you have a limited vocabulary for talking about emotions, then your ability to describe *and therefore be conscious of* emotions will be limited too. Building the vocabulary builds the ability to be aware. This is why teams that have a taboo on talk about emotions can't handle them very well when they arise.

Cognitive bias comes into play as well. The rational brain tries to interpret what's happening in the body, to make sense of it. Barrett tells the story of a college date where she thought she was falling for the person she was having dinner with…only to find later that her strange feelings came from a violent case of the flu she was developing. Learning to interpret the signals of the body clearly and without presuppositions is a key skill in navigating the waters of emotion.

Reactive brain and tribal brain

When you are confronted with a threat, you instinctively give your own safety as an individual the top priority. This individual reactivity can be a serious challenge for working as a team. When individuals are reactive, their capacity to use other habits (stable attention, connectedness, and open-mindedness) is seriously compromised. But in particular the reactive brain stimulates the tribal brain and brings out its worst tendencies. Fear induces not just a physiological and psychological response (as we shall see), but also a heightening of the kinds of tribal responses we explored in Chapter Two. Gaining greater awareness of your reactive brain is vital for managing the tribal impulse so you can build bridges with others and stay connected.

STEP FOUR: UNDERSTAND THE CORE PRACTICE

Pay attention to your reactions

Like cognitive bias, the fight-flee-freeze reaction is part of your system, and its basic wiring isn't really susceptible to much change. Given that, what can you do to work productively with your reactivity?

Bringing your patterns of reactivity into your awareness takes some skill and attention. Reactions come at inconvenient times and arise from the body in ways that are uncomfortable by definition. But the habit of stable attention you learned in Chapter One gives you a solid observation platform. The ability to pay attention to what's happening right here and right now, applied to your emotional experience, creates the necessary space to step back and notice what's happening without judgments.

There are two crucial aspects to paying attention to your reactions. First is noticing the body sensations that let you know you're having a reactive response. And second is gaining more awareness of the labels you apply to those sensations. Let's look at these two aspects in more detail.

Paying attention to body sensations

Your brain gets three kinds of information from the world. Most
well-known is "perception," the input you get from seeing,
hearing, smelling, tasting and touching the outside world. You
also get input from your body's movement and effort; this is
called "proprioperception" or "kinesthesia." The third kind of
information is "interoception": the physical sensations that come
to your brain from inside your body. Of the three, interoception is
by far the murkiest and least precise. If you've ever had the
experience of "referred pain" (a sensation in your body that
seems to be coming from one place but actually has its source
somewhere else) you know how confusing these body sensations
can be.

When interoception reaches your brain, your brain seeks to make
some sense of what's going on. If the experience is vivid enough,
the course is clear: "Call 911!" "Head for the bathroom!" "Scratch
that itch!" But when interoception is communicating body
reactions to the complicated stresses and subtle threats of
everyday life, its communications are much less clear. Make no
mistake: the queasy and tense sensations you feel when you walk
into a difficult meeting are affecting your brain. But if you don't
observe those sensations, you can't observe the cognitive impact.
Acquiring a basic vocabulary of the ways your body
communicates to you—your heartbeat, your sweat glands, your
gut, the muscles in your neck and shoulders—makes it easier to

bring the subtler forms of interoception to awareness. A few more examples are shown in the diagram below.[43]

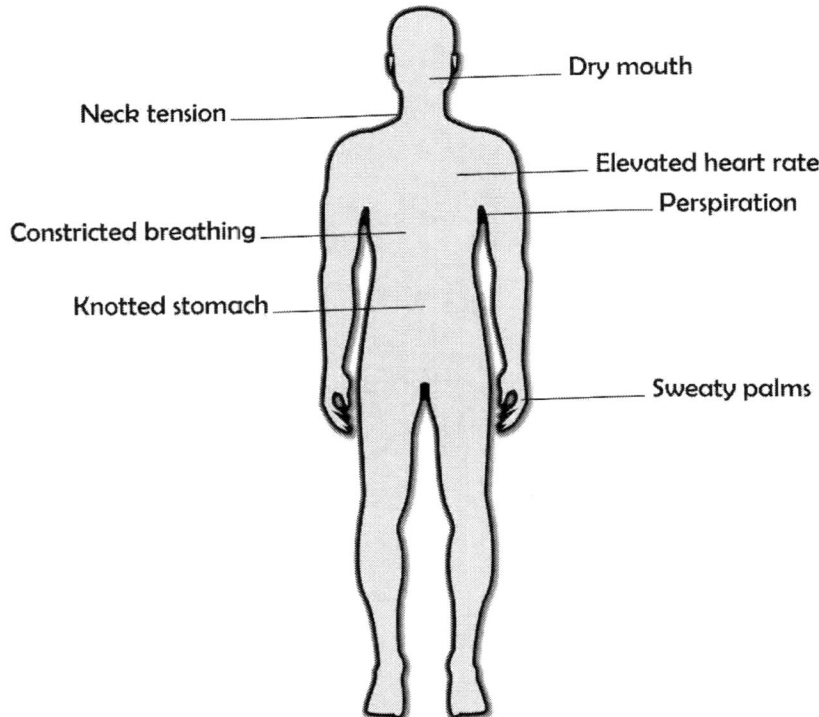

Neck tension

Dry mouth

Elevated heart rate

Perspiration

Constricted breathing

Knotted stomach

Sweaty palms

Noticing this information coming to you from your body is the first key to paying attention to emotional reactions.

Paying attention to labels

The second element of paying attention to your emotions is to notice the labels you apply to those body sensations. If the only word you have to describe the sensation of a pounding heart and rapid breathing is "anger"—then your experience will be angry a lot of the time. If you don't have any language at all for a subtle sense of unease in your gut, then your brain will respond to the circumstance unconsciously, and probably in a less-than-helpful way. If you can start to peer more carefully at a body sensation and find more precise words for the thoughts it stirs up, like "regretful because it's Francine's last day and I didn't get a chance to say goodbye," "disappointed that I wasn't taken more seriously," or "uneasy about what Bob will say," your experience is also more precise. You can make more conscious choices about what to do. You can experience your emotions in detail, as an ongoing sequence of body sensations and labels rather than an overwhelming tidal wave or an unconscious but powerful riptide.

For example, the following labels might be applied to a single generalized sensation, "tension": anxious, cranky, distressed, distraught, edgy, fidgety, frazzled, irritable, jittery, nervous, overwhelmed, restless, stressed out.[44] Each one could lead to significantly different interpretations of what's causing the tension, and what to do about it.

As with any aspect of language, your personal experience strongly colors your associations with the labels you apply. If "humiliated" or "disgusted" is a word that has certain resonances for you, those resonances will be invoked when you apply that word to a current experience. Part of making conscious choices about labels is your awareness of these associations. Carefully investigate them. When an association arises, is it warranted? Is what your co-worker just did really equivalent to what happened to you on prom night, or with your last boss?

Core Practice: Pay attention to your reactions

Even if you can't observe your emotional reactions in the moment (let's face it, that's really hard to do), when you step back and observe what happened, the chaotic jumble starts to untangle and you can make more sense of it. You're neither in denial about your reactivity, nor overwhelmed by it. Just noticing.

You can use the practice of present-moment, non-judgmental awareness—together with a cultivated ability to notice body sensations and the language you use to describe those sensations—to direct your attention to your emotional reactions. At first it can be helpful to notice your reactions to things that happened in the past (even minor incidents like some bad driving behavior you've observed). Over time it becomes easier to notice reactions as they are happening.

Here are some experiments to try.

Experiment: Notice a Sensation

Close your eyes and see if you can identify a physical sensation coming from within your body. Just let your attention settle wherever there's something going on: neck? shoulders? stomach? chest? mouth? When you have settled on a sensation, without desire or aversion and staying in the present moment, investigate that sensation. It's as though you're walking around it, gently assessing its nature and qualities, seeing where it's painful or tight or stuck. Again, no judgments: your task is just to notice the nature of this sensation with clarity.

Maintaining stable attention on a body sensation, especially if it's an uncomfortable one, might be difficult at first. If your attention drifts away, gently bring it back and continue exploring. The purpose of this experiment is to put you in touch with bodily information that impacts your awareness, your state of mind, and your choices. If spending time paying attention to your body is unfamiliar to you, notice that unfamiliarity with kindness. There is no right way to do this, and each of us approaches our experience of body in a different way. Remember this exercise is simply a first step toward improving your state of mind, your capacity to think clearly, and your ability to stay attuned to the people you work with.

The point of the next experiment is to notice your brain's labelling activity with curiosity. If you find you're resistant, or bored, or confused, just notice that, let it go, and return your attention to the activity.

Experiment: Labeling

Close your eyes and come back to the sensation you were just working with. Do you find yourself applying an emotional label to that sensation? Is it a version of one of the four basic emotions: "mad, sad, glad, afraid?" Something else going on with your body? Spend a few moments investigating the meaning you're applying to the sensation. If nothing comes clearly to mind, just notice the absence of meaning. Is there a label waiting to be applied that you're not yet aware of?

Before you begin the next experiment, remember emotional experiences occur on a broad spectrum of intensity. For this experiment it's best to choose experiences of relatively low intensity so you can investigate them in more detail.

Experiment: Recalling an Emotion

Bring to mind a recent experience when you felt afraid, or joyful, or angry, or sad. Close your eyes and see if you can recall the physical sensations that went along with that experience. While remaining aware that you're not having that experience now, can you identify precisely where in your body those sensations were located? Now consider the label you applied to that experience. As you reflect on it now, consider whether there's a more precise term you might apply.

There's a lot of variation in the ways humans experience emotions. Factors like culture, family background, and personal experience play an enormous role. On top of that, emotions are fluid and changeable. You could do the experiments above every day for a month, and each day your experience could be dramatically different. The practices in this chapter will give you a chance to explore your emotions, and especially your reactive emotions, with some consistency.

An image of self-awareness: the moment of waking up

Our emotional experience is very closely tied to our sense of identity. Here's an image to experiment with. It may help you step back from identifying with your emotions so you can observe them in a non-judgmental way.

Experiment: Waking Up

Imagine you have just awakened from a refreshing nap. You've been off in dreamland for a while, detached from

your body's sensations and the meaning your brain
attaches to those sensations. Notice the sensations in your
body as though they are new to you—you're just now
realizing what your head feels like, and your neck and
shoulders, your mouth, your gut and all the rest of you.
Next, again as though you're just waking up, notice the
labels your brain is applying to your newly awakened
self: "I'm looking forward to today," "I'm dreading
today"—whatever it might be. Step back from that brain
activity and notice the labels being applied. When you
were sleeping, none of those labels applied. What does it
mean that you are applying them now?

Use the micropractices in the table below to turn these
experiments into practical behavioral change over time. The
common theme of all these practices is to pay attention to the
sources of reactive emotions: body sensations and the labels you
apply to those sensations.

STEP FIVE: BUILD THE HABIT

Cultivating the habit of self-awareness

Becoming more self-aware of your emotional experiences, and
particularly your reactions, comes about by sustained practice
over time. Choose one or more of these micropractices and do it
every day. See page 17 for more about building habits.

Self-Awareness Micropractices

Pay Attention to Body Sensations, page 187

Pay Attention to What Triggers You, page 190

Pay Attention to Team Emotions, page 192

Pay Attention to Psychological Safety, page 196

What to expect as you build the habit

If you're under pressure, there are a lot of opportunities for reactivity. The last thing you need is another source of pressure, in the form of an expectation that you won't ever be reactive! When you perceive threat, your body and mind go into a reactive state—that is a given of your human and biological nature. The aim in cultivating self-awareness is to help you observe yourself with curiosity, openness, and even a little kindness. Achieving greater self-understanding is a valuable outcome in its own right.

An important but secondary goal is to begin to reduce the duration and the impact of your reactions, and to give you relatively more control over them. Particularly if you can engage in practices that involve your team, your self-awareness will tick up noticeably, and you will probably see some of those secondary benefits as well. When reactivity gets the best of you (and it will), take note of it, pay attention with a curious mind, and continue your investigation.

The Post-Mortem Meeting (continued)

Terra has just settled into her desk after the emotional intelligence workshop Alice had recommended. She's still musing on the potential of this material for her team when she sees that Padma has texted her: "Can you drop by my office, please?"

Text, not email—that can't be good. Terra's heart is pounding as she walks down the hall. "I hope I can remember that emotional intelligence stuff, because I have a feeling I'm going to need it."

Padma's look is grim when Terra walks in. Padma signals for her to close the door behind her.

"I'm afraid I have some bad news. Carlos has decided that Li Hua needs to go. To be honest, he's really pissed about this latest incident. The fact that we didn't do a better job of protecting data integrity is just not acceptable. And he holds Li Hua responsible—he doesn't like her passive attitude."

Terra is shocked. Of all the scenarios she imagined in the last five minutes, this was the last thing she expected. She can feel her heart racing, her stomach clenching, a swirl of intensity rising. Angry words are queuing up in her brain, ready to spill out: "That is so totally unfair! How can he blame Li Hua?" But instead, she remembers to take a pause, to notice the sensations first before responding. "OK, just a

minute, Padma—let me just take that in." (Micropractice: Pay
Attention to Body Sensations)

Thirty minutes later, Terra is back at her desk. She is a bit shaken, but
grateful she was able to manage the wave of her emotions while in
Padma's office. She was able to tell Padma in no uncertain terms that
she is angry—she feels Carlos's decision is unfair—but she stayed clear
and calm as she did so. She was able to hear more context from Padma
about what's going on with Carlos, including the pressure he's under
from the CEO and the board, and could listen with a certain amount of
empathy. After talking further about the incident and what was behind
it, Padma agrees with Terra that they should get more information
before making a decision about Li Hua.

As a result, Terra has another challenging conversation to negotiate.
Padma has asked her to attend a meeting with Carlos and Li Hua that
afternoon. "I don't think this is going to be easy," Padma told her. "But
it's best if we can get it all out on the table. I don't think Li Hua is safe.
But we'll find out."

Still feeling steamed, Terra takes a walk on her lunch break, and
considers how this meeting will go. "There are so many things about
this situation that are so typical. I'm sure George is pulling strings
behind the scenes to get rid of Li Hua. Li Hua is a woman, and Asian,
and I can't help but think that's part of it, too. Li Hua kept trying to tell
everyone about the risks, but no-one would listen to her. And now she's
being blamed? So unfair!" How many times has Terra seen this same
behavior? How many times has she suffered from similar situations
herself? "But," she reminds herself, "this situation is not those

situations. There are things about this that make me mad, but if I'm going to be a leader on this team, I need to stay focused on what's happening now and avoid getting tripped up by what happened in the past." (Micropractice: Pay Attention to What Triggers You)

Partly because Terra has prepared herself, the meeting goes better than expected—and Li Hua's job is saved. Terra is able to defend Li Hua's actions calmly, and she manages to avoid blaming George for causing trouble. When Carlos makes a comment about "women who don't speak up," Terra is able to let go of her resentment. She says calmly, "This has nothing to do with gender—it's about working together with trust and fairness," and keeps the conversation focused on what needs to happen next.

Terra is hoping the team can put this unpleasant bump in the road behind them. But when she walks into the next cross-functional team meeting—the first meeting after the post-mortem—she can tell things are not right. Li Hua has her head down and is carefully studying her phone. Not typical behavior. George sits on the other side of the room with his arms folded and appears to be annoyed. "Uh oh," Terra thinks. "Li Hua is fleeing, and George is ready for a fight. Is this left over from the post-mortem? Or did word about George's 'failed coup' get out? We're going to have to do something about this. Just not right now," she decides as she writes the meeting agenda on the whiteboard.

After the meeting Terra goes right to Padma's office. "We can't just ignore the emotions of this situation," Terra tells her. "Not only are Li Hua and George more alienated than ever, we have a lot of items from the post-mortem that's not going to be easy to sort through."

"Time for another one of your workshops?" Padma asks.

"Exactly what I was thinking," Terra replies. "We can bring some of this emotional intelligence stuff into the way our team works together. As you know, we've made a lot of progress—but until we get this piece in place, we'll keep tripping over our reactions."

Given the fraught atmosphere, Terra has real concerns about doing too much in the workshop she schedules the next week. "Emotions are never easy, and things are tense right now," she thinks. "We're going to take baby steps." Keeping the conversation objective, rooted in brain science and the practical reality that everyone has a body, she makes the case for acknowledging reactive emotions as part of the team's ongoing work. She doesn't confront George for his aggression, or Li Hua for her tendency to retreat. She simply lays out a plan for how the team can safely bring their reactions—and the impact of those reactions—into the way they work together. (Micropractice: Pay Attention to Team Emotions)

The last person Terra expects to see after the workshop is George. She stiffens as he approaches her cube. "Watch that reactivity, Terra," she tells herself. "Hi George," she manages to say. "Thanks for coming to the session today."

"I just want you to know I won't forget what you did," George says...and walks away.

"What was that about?" Terra wonders. "Did he like the workshop? Did he find out somehow that I spoke up for Li Hua? It's so hard to read him."

Terra looks, for the fiftieth time that week, at the photo of a beach in Maui tacked to her cube. "After I get back from Hawaii," she thinks, "I'll have to ask him about it." She closes her eyes and imagines blue skies and gentle surf. Peace, rest, and refuge. "Refuge," she thinks. "That's something that would make our whole team better. Maybe I can bring some of that back with me along with the macadamia nuts." (Micropractice: Pay Attention to Psychological Safety)

STEP SIX: KEEP IT RELEVANT

Change management

Self-awareness creates a nurturing environment where your team and your organization can grow a healthy and resilient culture. While this has many benefits, resilience is vital when you face the challenges of change. Let's look at how organizations and teams that cultivate healthy self-awareness are better equipped to navigate any organizational change initiative, including changes introduced by mergers and acquisitions.

Self-aware change management

Organizations facing change use a wide variety of change management frameworks.[45] There's one word that crops up consistently in all the different frameworks: resistance.

- In Kurt Lewin's change management model, the first step, "unfreeze," is focused on breaking down the status quo to show why it can't continue as it is. Why is this step necessary? Because of resistance to change.

- John Kotter's model for leading change includes steps for "Getting Everyone on Board and Reducing Friction and

Removing Obstacles." Why are these steps necessary? Because of resistance to change.

- In Jeffrey M. Hiatt's ADKAR model, the second letter "D" — Desire—is the key. To achieve change, you need to gain commitment. And, as Hiatt points out, the obstacle to commitment is resistance.
- Richard H. Thaler and Cass R. Sunstein's Nudge theory is entirely focused on the reality of resistance to change and the need to encourage people to adopt change incrementally.
- Three change management models (William Bridges' Transition model, a model based on the five stages of grief, and a model based on the work of family therapist Virginia Satir) are explicitly focused on the psychological reactions to change that individuals have—including resistance—and working with those reactions.

What's the common factor that lies underneath resistance to change? Fear. It turns out that organizational change takes us right back out to the savannah, with all our reactivity mechanisms fully engaged. You discover that something in your environment—large or small—is about to change. You experience a threat; your body generates reactive sensations (fighting, fleeing or freezing) as a result; your brain creates language to label the experience; and you are locked into a reactive response.

It's no wonder change management models take resistance seriously. But teams that put time and energy into developing their own self-awareness, as individuals and together, are much better equipped to work productively with their resistance. First, they have developed the ability to be aware of their physical reactions. Second, they understand themselves well enough to know what triggers them, what labels they apply when various flavors of threat arise, and what their patterns of reactivity are. Finally—and perhaps most importantly—they are comfortable as a team acknowledging the presence of emotional responses. Since a self-aware team is already in the habit of working with their reactivity, when change comes (however major, or formal, or chaotic, or scary) they have the tools they need to address any resistance that might arise.

A practice for better change management

All the Stable Attention micropractices will help you and your team navigate change with greater effectiveness. Here's one practice that's a good place to start:

 Working with resistance to change starts with body awareness. Use the micropractice Pay Attention to Body Sensations to help with this. Notice the clues of anxiety, fear, or resistance that arise in your body when you're confronted with new circumstances. When you and your team can be open about the physiological responses you're noticing, you're well on your way to having a genuine and productive conversation about what's coming and what you can do about it.

For several years I did technology planning and content development for a website that supported public library staff nationwide. There were a lot of librarians on the website team, and I came to admire and respect them, both professionally and as genuinely aware humans. The project involved a great deal of change, as technologies and partnerships and staffing and funding kept shifting around. As a team we got into the habit of singing songs (made-up words to the tune of popular songs) to describe whatever challenging circumstance we happened to run into. What I loved most about that practice was that the singing acknowledged the difficulty yet brought us right back into our bodies. After one of these songs, it always felt like the air was clearer and we were better able to face a challenge.

Self-awareness and integrating cultures

According to a survey of executives conducted by Bain & Company, the number one reason why mergers don't realize their expected value is a clash between the cultures of the merging companies.[46] A merger or an acquisition triggers the inherent tribalism woven into our cognitive apparatus (see Chapter Two for more on this). A key driver of the tribal behavior that thwarts attempts to integrate disparate cultures is emotional reactivity in response to a perception of threat.

Let's consider how staying self-aware can make every phase of integrating two organizations go more smoothly. We'll look at this from the perspective of an organizational or team leader, although everything below has its relevance for each person who's affected:[47]

Communicating: Poised over your keyboard, about to hit "Send" on an email announcing that your team or organization is going to be integrated with a group of strangers, an array of emotions flows through your body and mind: excitement, anxiety, doubt and more. You know that when you click that button and your team gets the note, those emotions are going to be greatly amplified. Your capacity to handle your own emotions and be aware of the emotions of others is vital, both to crafting that note in the right way and working with the response. It's only the first step of a long journey, but you want to get off on the right foot.

Retaining key people: After the announcement has gone out, everyone's experience of risk is heightened. Distractions abound. The tribal longing for belonging and fear of exclusion kicks in. Minds race ahead, envisioning all sorts of scenarios—usually based on limited information. You're going to have to make some tough decisions, and team members will have to make decisions too. Amidst all the swirl, you need to stay attentive to the fact that every thought and decision will be profoundly influenced by emotional experiences of all kinds. Being aware of your own emotions and the emotions of others, especially when every conversation is loaded with overtones of loyalty and loss, anxiety and disappointment, is essential. If you're intent on ensuring that the people you need to stick around will stick around, and that others (who—for whatever reason—are not so central to the organization's future needs) are being treated fairly and with respect, you're going to need that self-awareness every day.

Win hearts and minds: As we've seen in Chapter Three, positivity is an important practice, and this is particularly true in the face of change. But it would be disingenuous to suppose that managing change is just about talking up exciting possibilities. The unfortunate reality is that managing change is managing loss.[48] When two organizations merge, one organization's culture may be chosen for adoption, but ultimately everyone involved is going to lose something. It's important not to disregard the central emotional experience of loss, even as you remain positive and intent on the greater good you are seeking. As things you have loved and built start to change, you'll need to navigate your own emotions of grief, while at the same time remaining attentive to the distinctive flavors of grief that show up in those you work with.

A practice for better M&A integration

The Self-Awareness micropractices focus on working with the emotions of reactivity, the immediate twitch response to fight, flee or freeze. These skills of body awareness and self-understanding will help you work with the potent emotions that show up when organizations undergo profound change. But perhaps most crucial of all is improving the sense of psychological safety on your team. As challenging as this might seem when loss is on the horizon, remember psychological safety does not require any certainty about what will happen next. It has to do with what's happening now.

 Start now to build your team's psychological safety by explicitly calling for self-awareness, inclusivity, listening and speaking up (practice 4.4). No matter what the current level of psychological safety, it's well worth taking the time to make your team more resilient in the face of change.

I had the good fortune to work for several years at WRQ, a legendary Seattle software company that had the highest-quality organizational culture I've ever experienced. Much of that was thanks to the founder, Doug Walker, who was an instinctual purveyor of psychological safety long before the term existed. One key characteristic of the culture was an open invitation and encouragement for everyone to speak up. This invitation happened at weekly all-staff meetings. It happened in one-on-one meetings with Doug in his office. It happened in all kinds of team conversations. That doesn't mean it wasn't sometimes scary to say something controversial in front of Doug or a roomful of other people. But the invitation made all the difference.

NEXT STEPS
Keep Cultivating!

Taking baby steps, you can cover a lot of ground.

The cultural anthropologist Angeles Arrien describes healing as "a lifelong journey toward wholeness."[49] It's unlikely that you'll be with your current team for life—and yet you are, in an important sense, on a healing journey together. The challenges you face and the problems you solve will help your organization be more successful, but they have the very important additional benefit of moving you, your team, and your organizational culture closer to health and happiness.

My hope is that any changes you and your team make because of your encounter with this book, however small, are steps on that journey toward wholeness.

In the 1991 film *What About Bob,* Bill Murray plays a lovable neurotic who learns from his psychotherapist (played by Richard Dreyfuss) to take "baby steps": "Setting small reasonable goals for yourself one day at a time. One tiny step at a time." Bob is delighted to discover this technique and puts it to use right away: "Baby steps through the office…baby steps out the door…it works! It works!" By the end of the film, the "baby steps" have transformed Bob in entirely unexpected ways.

Cultivating the "baby steps" of paying attention takes some time and goes through different stages. As with any habit, at first you'll be amazed by the impact of your shift in awareness. Then after a while you'll get used to the difference and it won't seem amazing. If you stop doing the practices, the habit will atrophy. You'll vaguely notice you're missing something, but you won't be quite sure what it is.

Remember the four rules of building a habit on page 17. Here are a few additional suggestions to help you keep going.

1. **Be accountable to others.** Tell people in your life what you're doing and invite them to ask you periodically how it's going. If you're building the habits of paying attention as a team

activity, accountability happens naturally through the shared experience.

2. **Recognize the benefits and stay aware of them.** The more you can tie the practices to specific outcomes (for yourself and your career, for your team, for your organization) the more consistently you'll stick with them.

3. **Forgive yourself when you lapse.** There will be days and times when you don't do what you intended. Since the foundational practice is curious, open, noticing in the present moment...just apply that practice to the lapse. Without judgments, notice what happened, and consider why. Then let it go, adjust if needed, and resume the practice.

4. **Overcome your natural resistance to change.** There will be days when your sense of accountability and aspiration will run into conflict with laziness, boredom, annoyance, or rationalization—the attitudes and behaviors humans have always used to resist change. Be aware resistance will come. Acknowledge it when it crops up, and remind yourself why you're ready for something different.

The small actions you take to improve your attention today can make your team better: more attentive, more aware of each other and yourselves, and more thoughtful. Repeating these actions over time so they can grow into habits will lead you toward wholeness and sustained growth over time. You don't have to wait to make a plan or to find the right time or circumstances. By improving your ability to pay attention today, even a little bit, you can start making things better.

Epilogue

As Terra scans her email inbox the Monday morning after flying home from her Hawaiian vacation, her heart sinks just a bit. "Have we made any progress at all?" Her first read through her email inbox suggests not. George, Li Hua, Padma, and the rest of the gang seem to be up to their old tricks. And Terra is pretty sure that she herself will be fall into her old habits soon enough, probably long before her Hawaiian tan fades.

"It's the human brain at work," she thinks. "It just wants to do its thing."

At the cross-functional team meeting, it's clear that new pressures, new projects, and new customer demands are weighing on the group. A new set of organizational changes, coming soon, is adding to the stress. And yet, little encouraging things are happening too. George starts multitasking during the meeting—but then he stops, looks up sheepishly, and says, "This can wait. I want to make sure I hear what you're saying." On her way into the meeting room, both introverted Li Hua and overbearing George asks Terra about her vacation—and actually seems genuinely interested in what she has to say. Padma asks a couple of good questions during the meeting: curious questions, not ones she already knows the answer to. And when Padma fires a particularly challenging question at her, Terra is pleased to find that, although her heart jumps as it always does in that moment, she is able to notice the sensation and recover.

Terra considers the road ahead. "We're going to need to keep working at paying attention. Because the world is definitely not going to slow down."

MICROPRACTICES
Building the Habits of Attention

Establish consistent routines to cultivate flexibility.

This section includes 16 micropractices that you can use to build the habits of awareness. You can use the practices as is, or adapt them in any way that's useful, or use what you already know, or come up with your own. The important thing is to keep going! You'll find additional practices at www.jhanderson.biz.

STABLE ATTENTION

 Pay Attention to Your Breath

Use your breath as a reminder of stable awareness that's always available.

The Practice

1. Find a place where you can sit comfortably for two minutes The location doesn't have to be completely silent, or dark, or special in any way. Just a place where you can sit with your eyes closed and feel safe and undisturbed for two minutes. It could be your bedroom, or your lunchroom, or the lobby of your building. You can do this inside or outside.
2. Close your eyes.
3. Notice your breathing for two minutes.
    *   For this practice, there is no need to make any changes to how you breathe. The task is simply to notice how the breathing is happening.
    *   Notice where you feel the sensation of air moving in and out of your respiratory system. There are a lot of possibilities: nostrils, mouth, throat, upper chest, belly. All are involved to some degree—just notice where in your body the sensation of breathing is happening.
    *   Notice any movement in your body that is happening as a result of breathing. What are the muscles involved in breathing (from neck on down to diaphragm) doing?

What movements seem to be caused by the flow of air itself?

- As your investigation of your breath gets more detailed, you might notice some nuances. For example, you might tune in to that tiny microsecond at the end of each inhale and each exhale where your breath naturally pauses. You might subdivide each inbreath and each outbreath into five parts, and notice what happens in each part. How do the sensations change as your lungs gradually expand and contract through each moment of the breathing cycle?

4. When your mind wanders, gently bring it back. If your breathing changes as you observe it…just observe that too.

Background

Using your breath as an object of attention has many benefits. It's right there in the center of your body. You're breathing all the time, so it's always there to be noticed. And focusing on your breath lets you practice a shift of awareness without anyone else having a clue that you're doing it.

Your breathing is often the first clue that your attention is unsettled. If you observe that your breathing has gotten very shallow, or that you haven't noticed you're breathing for a while, that's a pretty good indication something is distracting you.

See if you can keep up the practice of noticing your breath for two minutes in an undisturbed place every day for a week or two. Be on the lookout for changes, and if you notice even the slightest improvement in your attention or focus, be sure to celebrate! If you miss a day for whatever reason, be kind to yourself and get back to it. Slowly, gradually, let this practice find its way into your life.

See if you can start noticing your breath for brief periods during the day. Take a breath or two before you turn to your email inbox, or before you make a call, or while everyone's getting settled into a meeting or a conference call. If you're especially wound up, take four or five breaths—just 30 seconds. Once you've done the breathing practice for a while, you can use it as a touchstone for recovering your attention in all kinds of situations. In fact, attention is always just a breath away.

Find an Anchor Point

Establish a point of stability in the midst of everyday pressures.

The Practice

1. Choose an object in your workplace as a reminder to pause and come back to the present moment. Use an object you see many times a day.

   - This object could be something personally meaningful, like a picture of a loved one on your desk.
   - It could be a completely random item that serves its function by its very ordinariness.
   - You might even put a pink sticky note in an obscure corner of your work environment, as a reminder to recover your attention.

2. Each time you see this object, do a brief micro-practice like taking two or three breaths, bringing your attention to your feet, or repeating a brief calming phrase that is meaningful to you.

3. Set an intention that whenever this object comes into view, you'll notice it and do an attention reset.
   - When you do notice and reset, celebrate.
   - When you walk right by your anchor point without noticing it because you're distracted, be kind to yourself, notice the lapse, and reset your intention.
   - After a week or two you'll get to the point where *not* noticing your anchor point would start to seem strange,

like not putting on your seatbelt when you get into a car or leaving the house without your wallet.

Background

I was climbing the stairs in my office building one day and noticed a small crumpled gum wrapper lying on a step. Should I pick it up, or leave it there? I decided on the latter and continued to climb. The next day the wrapper was still there. I started to get curious about how long it would last. After a few days, I started to view its restful state, there on the step, as a symbol of my own intention to be more clear, focused and centered at work. That gum wrapper became my going-to-work meditation for quite some time—until the day a janitor or some other conscientious person took it away.

Whatever your work environment (office, or home, or anywhere in between), it is full of little details that have the potential to bring you back to present-moment awareness. Start by focusing on one anchor point so you get in the habit of recovering your attention while you're at work. You can expand from there, adding more anchor points in conference rooms, your boss's office, the bathroom, and more. I have a particular fondness for stairwells (in one of my jobs I was fortunate enough to have a few chanting friends—we'd sing together at lunchtime in a very resonant stairwell space), but lunchrooms, hallways, lobbies, and many other spaces have equal potential. (You can use my free e-book *The Mindful Office* for some more ideas.[50])

Pay Attention in Meetings

Reinvigorate your meetings with common-sense methods of improving attention.

The Practice

1. **Notice what's happening.** No matter how great or terrible a meeting is, you are always free to step back and observe what's happening. That will free you to really see what's going on and make good decisions about what to do in response.

2. **Create an environment conducive to attention.** Clear away any detritus from previous meetings, empty the trash, open a window if you can. Make sure there's enough room for everyone to sit or stand comfortably and equitably. If some or all participants are on a phone conference or video line, take care to ensure they can be seen and heard.

3. **Set a clear intention.** Send an agenda, meeting objectives and timing for each item to all participants beforehand—even if it's a daily standup meeting. Taking five minutes to review where things stand and what's percolating helps maintain a clear intention. This obvious and commonsense tactic has surprising potential to dramatically improve the quality of attention of a whole team, without them even quite realizing why it's happening.

4. **Set ground rules.** Consider a no-device policy,[51] respect the agenda, avoid side conversations—and start and end on time. As with step 3, this simple act of team discipline can have extraordinarily beneficial consequences.

5. **Begin and end the meeting with attention.** At the beginning
    of a meeting, give each attendee 10 seconds to answer the
    question, "On a scale of 1-10, how present are you right
    now?" and briefly explain why. If someone gives themselves
    a low score because they are distracted by a challenge at
    home or an urgent demand they have to address right after
    the meeting, it's important for everyone to know. And having
    been heard, that person can be a little more present. At the
    end, have each person say one word that expresses their state
    of mind as a result of the meeting. That one word will reveal
    a lot about what happened, and what needs to happen next

6. **Document the meeting.** Capture what was discussed, what
    was agreed to, and what issues are still open—even for a
    quick daily status meeting. This is another common-sense
    practice, but meeting notes have great power to bring clarity
    and expose what's still murky. Writing in general is, in fact, a
    very important resource for building stable attention.

7. **Keep habitual meetings fresh.** In recurring meetings (like
    standup or weekly status meetings) it's easy to let familiarity
    take over and dull the edge of present-moment awareness.
    These repeating meetings function as rituals. And like any
    ritual, they are most powerful when they provide a
    framework for doing the important work, but do not deaden
    the work itself. When alert people engage in intentional ritual
    for a specific purpose, the collective focused energy can break
    down almost any barrier. The trick is to find the right balance
    between order and spontaneity.

- Rituals provide the order. It's 10 o'clock, and the standup meeting is happening, and everyone is there for the purpose of sharing their progress and the obstacles they are facing. Without order, the random demands of the everyday will chew up time and attention. Ritual provides the necessary context for information to be shared and connections to be made.

- The spontaneity comes from the awake, present-moment awareness each individual brings to the ritual. Without this quality of attention, the ritual quickly degenerates into a formulaic routine that checks the "standup happened today" box but doesn't add any real value.

8. **Use "yes, and..."** While each individual has a responsibility to bring their own presence and present-moment awareness to the ritual activity, skillful facilitation can help. Practices like having each participant preface their comments with "yes, and" can create an atmosphere of positivity and acceptance. But keep in mind that any spontaneity-inducing practice can quickly be absorbed by a ritual meeting that is stuck in deadness. When "yes, and" becomes "yes, and now shut up," the formula has become dead and the spirit of lively attention has been lost.

Background

A recent survey of 182 senior managers in a range of industries found that 65% said meetings keep them from completing their own work, 71% said meetings are unproductive and inefficient, 64% said meetings come at the expense of deep thinking, and

62% said meetings miss opportunities to bring the team closer together. Research like this has been happening for decades, and yet the amount of time teams spend in meetings has been on the rise.[52]

"We have too many meetings!" It's a common enough cry, but as the findings above suggest, that isn't really the problem. Meetings are a tremendous opportunity for connection. The deeper issue is that we have too many ineffective and time-wasting meetings—too many meetings where attention is scarce and distraction is everywhere. There is nothing groundbreaking about the practices above they are common-sense measures that have been widely adopted and proven to make meetings better.

Like any practice, establishing a rhythm where attention is a consistent feature of the way meetings happen takes time, and intention, and patience. All the features of any successful practice are required. Celebrate successes. Be kind and start again when failure happens. And keep it up until the behavior you want starts to become a habit.

Pay Attention as a Team

Agree together to call attention to team distractions the moment they occur.

The Practice

1. Agree on a keyword, phrase, or signal sound any team member can use to call attention to the possibility that the group has gotten distracted.
   - Find a word that's value-neutral and memorable, like "rooster" or "VCR."
   - You could use whistling, a phrase from a song, or an animal sound.
   - The specific word doesn't matter, as long as everyone knows what it means.

2. At any point in team conversations, any team member can initiate the attention-recovery protocol by using the agreed-upon signal. The signal says, "It seems to me we have gotten lost in thought—we've wandered away from our intention for this meeting."

3. Using a quick thumbs-up, thumbs-down vote, the team assesses whether distraction is what is happening. (There may be differences of opinion about this. If there's no consensus, the conversation continues.)

4. If there is a consensus that distraction is happening, the team pauses the conversation for a moment. This pause can be very brief, as little as 10 seconds—the space of one breath.

5. During the pause, each team member does a simple activity (feeling their feet, looking at an object out the window, taking

a deep breath) to recover attention and come back to the present moment.

6. After the pause, the conversation resumes. If necessary, the group may want to evaluate if something needs to change. Was the pause enough to get the conversation back on track? Is something deeper needed, like the presence of someone who's not currently in the room, or further investigation, or a more substantial break?

Background

When your team is under the gun, time is short and there's a lot of work to do, it seems counterintuitive to slow the conversation down. When a team is struggling to find focus and direction, it seems like more talking is the best way to figure things out. But in both cases less talking may be the perfect remedy.

The purpose of this practice is to introduce space into your team's conversations. You're not asking team members to make dramatic changes to the way they function—just allow for a little room to breathe. Like the Lean concept of "minimum viable product," you might think of this practice as "minimum viable attention." Without unduly disrupting the flow, without taking too much time away from the conversations that need to happen, team members are gently reminding one another that attention matters. "If attention isn't happening," the protocol says, "let's agree to stop right here and right now until it's recovered."

CONNECTEDNESS

 ## Pay Attention to Your Humanity

Broaden and deepen the definition of "us."

The Practice

1. Each day choose a person on your immediate or extended team, and set an intention to discover something about their human experience for the purpose of building your connection with them.

2. While it's always possible to discover things indirectly, for example through social media or by asking other people, the connection will be much stronger and clearer if you ask directly. Just tell them you're looking to build more team cohesiveness and would like to understand a little more about them.

Team activities are a golden opportunity to do this practice, particularly if the following conditions are in place:

- The team activity is primarily focused on building connections, not dominated by a distracting focal point (like a sports activity or karaoke).

- The team activity is equally welcoming of old-timers and newcomers, extraverts and introverts.

- The music or ambient noise is not so loud that you can't hear what other people are saying.

- The environment and activities are designed so everyone has an opportunity to participate in conversation and circulate. "Table topics"—questions each person at the table answers—

or "speed dating" formats are great ways to make this happen.

Background

In nearly thirty years of working on teams, I've been to a whole lot of team-building social events. A few that stand out: a combo kayak-trip-and-baby-shower, a role-playing murder mystery, an eagle-watching expedition to the Skagit River (over 250 eagles spotted in one cold and wet afternoon), and a medieval feast in an ancient German castle. And of course, the usual complement of more mundane activities: bowling, ropes courses, cooking, eating, dancing, and singing together.

With very few exceptions, though, I have to think hard to remember the details of these events. What I remember most are the moments when I connected with the people I worked with. Sometimes it was in the context of what we were doing, as in feeling the weight of the other team members on a giant teeter-totter during a ropes course, or seeing how someone else chopped vegetables or made pancakes when we were cooking together. But much of the time it was the interesting tidbits I learned about people's families, and backgrounds, and the way they thought about things as a result of the ordinary conversations we had, doing whatever extraordinary thing we were doing. Fun is good. Creative and unusual is good. But connecting as humans is what will make your team strong.

Expand Your Circle of Concern

Take care of yourself...but don't stop there.

The Practice

1. Consider the members of your work team, particularly those who are part of an extended team, such as people in other departments, business partners in your organization, external partners, and customers.
2. Focus your attention on someone on your extended team who falls outside your natural circle of concern, and with whom you want or need to build a connection.
    *   This will be a person you don't think about every day, and whom you find it hard to keep in mind naturally.
    *   The issue might be distance, or a very different type of job, or a very different (or even a difficult) personality.
3. Simply set the intention to expand your circle of concern to include this person.
4. No action is required: you don't need to change your mind or your judgments. Just expand the circle, and notice that it includes a person it didn't include before.
5. Depending on where your circle of concern needs to grow, you might try this practice with a different person every day, or come back to the same person repeatedly to build a strong connection with them.

The following is an alternate form of this practice that consciously lowers the barriers that separate you from other people.[53] First think of a person close to you, whether a loved one, a family member, or someone you enjoy most of the time. Call them to mind and intend the following for them. You can do this silently or out loud.

- May you be safe.
- May you be happy.
- May you be well.
- May you live with ease.

Repeat the same four intentions for someone you feel neutral about. Then repeat them again, for someone you find challenging. Conclude by repeating them again for your whole team, or your whole company, or even everyone on the planet.

Background

In her book *Technology and the Virtues*,[54] Shannon Vallor draws on classical Greek, ancient Chinese, and Buddhist principles to lay out a framework for ethical action in the rapidly changing 21st century technological environment. A key principle is "expanding your circle of concern." As humans we have a natural capacity to care and feel concern for those close to us. By extending that same capacity more broadly, we build a web of connectedness and trust.

It starts by understanding where your natural sense of concern lies: with your friends, with your family, with your community, with the environment or the cause that matters most to you. The practice is to take that same sense of concern and apply it to others who don't naturally seem to fit within that circle. As you expand the circle, you don't have to feel concern to the same *degree*, only the same *kind* of concern. You recognize those normally outside your circle as worthy of concern. In the course of time your words and actions might change—but the point of this practice is just to expand the circle.

Pay Attention to the Other Point of View

Form a well-developed, conscious and articulate understanding of someone else's point of view.

The Practice

1. Choose a specific person you work with who has seemed particularly difficult or challenging, and whom you want to build a stronger connection with.

2. First check out your Theory of Mind by making notes on the following:

    *   How would you describe the factors that lead them into a perspective different from yours?

    *   What job responsibilities and pressures do they face?

    *   What do you know about their background and their personal life?

    *   What unvalidated assumptions are you making about them?

3. Then do some perspective-taking by imagining yourself in their shoes, and make notes on the following:

    *   What does it feel like to be in their situation?

    *   What does the world look like, seen through their eyes?

    *   What do *you* look like, seen through their eyes?

4. Use the next micropractice, Pay Attention to Your Perceptions of Others, to validate your findings.

Background

"If you want to understand someone, walk a mile in their shoes." It's a proverb that rings true and is a key component of team trust-building. The proverb encapsulates two powerful concepts: Theory of Mind and perspective-taking.

Remember that Theory of Mind is our ability to recognize other people have a different point of view than we do. They look at problems and possibilities from inside themselves. Their whole constellation of life experience—education, family background, and more—gives them different ways of looking at things than I have. Though Theory of Mind is essential, by itself it's not enough. For while it gives us the conceptual framework—the theory—for understanding someone else's point of view, it doesn't lead us into their experience.

Perspective-taking goes beyond theory, and into the act of imagination that allows you to step into another person's shoes and take a walk. Of course, your feet won't fit perfectly into the shoes—perspective-taking will never be entirely comfortable—but you get valuable information unavailable any other way. You notice the contours of the sole, the shape of the heel, the way your weight shifts. Perhaps most importantly, perspective-taking humbles you. It doesn't take long to realize the other person's world contains as much experience and nuance as yours.

Pay Attention to Your Perceptions of Others

Use simple questions to validate what you see and how you interpret it.

The Practice

1. Choose a person on your team you want to build a better connection with.

2. While you're reading email messages from that person, or in a meeting together, notice when you come to a definite conclusion about something they are experiencing (their thoughts, their feelings, their judgments or attitudes).

3. If possible, write down what you notice.
   - This step can help you clarify your own perceptions.
   - You might also use some material from the previous micropractice, Pay Attention to the Other Point of View.

4. As soon thereafter as possible, ask the person to meet with you briefly, in person or over the phone (email or chat is not the right communication medium for what comes next).

5. When you meet, tell them what you noticed. While it may be necessary to edit your thoughts to some degree, make what you share an honest statement.
   - You might use the format "You seem _____. Am I reading that right? Is that accurate?"
   - Asking a third person doesn't accomplish the goal here. The aim is to ask the person directly.

6. Listen carefully to their response. Recognize that depending on the person and their relationship with you, you may not

always get a straight, accurate, or useful answer. Even if there isn't a useful answer in the moment, you've started a conversation that can yield insight over time.

7. Thank them for their time and the information.

8. As your team's sense of connectedness and safety grows, you can begin to use this practice while conversations are happening (one-to-one or during meetings).

Background

The city of Seattle has grown nearly 20% between 2010 and 2018 (when I'm writing this). This change has all sorts of consequences, but the one that may affect me the most is a collective breakdown in the civility of driving behavior. When I moved here from San Francisco in 1989, Seattle driving customs seemed almost quaint. Getting through a 4-way stop seemed to take forever, as drivers gestured politely to each other to proceed. Those days are gone, and aggressive driving seems to be the new normal.

Driving in the city gives me plenty of opportunity to reflect on my habit of jumping to conclusions about intentions or states of mind of other drivers. Without access to words, or body language, or facial expressions, all I get is the roar of an engine and a glimpse of a sleek fiberglass or a rusted auto body.

It's challenging to use perspective-taking to drive a mile in that driver's car: where is that person going, and why? What is that person's state of mind? What just happened to them? Do they have a spouse and kids? What do their parents think about them?

What work do they do in the world? All those fascinating questions, and the human richness that comes with the answers, are collapsed into a moment of judgment: I assume I'm seeing an example of bad behavior and a fully fleshed-out story (entirely made up by me) of carelessness and disrespect.

That whole thought process of making sense out of another's actions takes place with regularity in your work relationships too. People are making up stories about you, and you're making up stories about them. These stories are more informed than our road-rage stories, based as they are on what we hear and see, and on our past experience working together. Nevertheless, they are usually unconfirmed, and as a result can be pretty inaccurate.

While you will never know what made the driver of that black Corvette do what he did at the last intersection, that is not the case with work interactions. There is a way for you to find out: ask. You're letting the other person know that they are having an effect on you—it's a communication to them—but also giving them the opportunity to fill in your story with some facts about their current state of mind. The offer will not always be taken, and that's OK. If not, you've established a basis for trying again another day when the person might be ready for a more open conversation. If so, you've opened up a channel of communication that can lead to a much more accurate view of that person's world. And that beats jumping to conclusions.

OPEN-MINDEDNESS

 Pay Attention to the Good

Deliberately focus on taking in the good, and deliberately celebrate.

The Practice

At a team meeting, before you dig into the agenda, allocate two-and-a-half minutes to wholeheartedly celebrating one recent accomplishment.

1. First two minutes: identify the accomplishment.
    - Begin by having one team member name an accomplishment. Make this a rotating responsibility for each meeting. Whatever is said, that's what you're going to celebrate.
    - What really worked, and why did it work?
    - If team members hold any reservations that make it difficult for them to fully embrace the accomplishment, consider: What would it be like to set those reservations aside for 30 seconds? You can always come back to those reservations later.

2. Last 30 seconds: Use Rick Hanson's HEAL methodology (from *Hardwiring Happiness*[55]) to truly savor the accomplishment:
    - Have a positive experience. Really notice when something good (a personal or team success, however large or small) happens.

- Enrich it. Stay with the positive experience for five to ten seconds. That sustained "yay" may feel like an eternity, but it's very powerful.
- Absorb it. Experience the positive sensation sinking into you, like hot tea or a good Scotch.
- Link positive and negative material (optional – will require a bit of extra time). Tie the positive sensation to something challenging that's going on. Use the positivity to balance and bring clarity, energy and possibility to that difficult situation.

Background

Mistakes made by collaborative teams are painful. The phrase "post-mortem" sometimes used to describe retrospective meetings reveals just how catastrophic the consequences of bad decisions can be. In the software development world, build-checking tools like the Siren of Shame[56] and LightBuild,[57] designed to give instant feedback when something goes wrong, rightly emphasize the need for accountability and responsiveness to errors. Anywhere the stakes are high, from sales to finance to leadership, such unforgiving feedback mechanisms are needed.

But there's one thing that matters more than avoiding errors, and that is seeing what is really true. And to do that, you need to address two brain tendencies.

The first tendency is that we prefer an oversimplified story that is either all cyclones or all rainbows. That simplicity is a good survival mechanism in a lot of contexts—it's very efficient—but doesn't come to terms with the complex reality of collaborative team work. What's really true is that both failures and successes happen--all the time. To have an accurate view of reality, one that enables you to take action to optimize what's working and fix what's not working, you need to see both good and bad.

The second tendency is negativity bias: our preference to see problems. This means that if you're reducing the world to either cyclones or rainbows, you're much more likely to pick cyclones.

The remedy is really quite simple, almost too simple: you and your team need to celebrate your successes. The reason to do this is not to sweep problems under the rug, or to be overly optimistic. You celebrate successes to overcome the bias toward negativity and to shift the focus from all-bad to both-good-and-bad.

In my role as a program manager delivering complex enterprise initiatives, I have been as skeptical as anyone else about too much "happy-clappy" celebration. But the fact is that celebration is essential to keeping a team's view of reality in balance.

Rick Hanson's book *Hardwiring Happiness* details a practice he calls "taking in the good."[58] It's the choice to allow yourself to see the positive dimensions of any circumstance. "Taking in the good" means consciously and deliberately focusing your attention on what is positive, expansive, and fortunate in your environment.

As you start to take in the good, some behavior changes might ensue. It might mean complimenting your co-workers when they do a good job. Or it could mean giving five pieces of positive feedback for every one negative. (This 5:1 positive:negative feedback ratio, known as the Losada Ratio,[59] has been shown to correlate to high business performance.) But the first and most important step is to take in the good yourself. When you experience something positive, take the time to really soak it in. It's the perfect antidote for negativity bias.

Pay Attention to the Planning Fallacy

Notice your tendency to oversimplify--especially when oversimplification is convenient.

The Practice

1. Allocate five minutes in a meeting to take an honest look at a current plan for work your team is doing. This could be a two-week sprint plan or a six-month "agilefall" schedule.

2. How accurate are your current timelines and estimates? Have each team member give a rating from 1 (not accurate at all) to 10 (very accurate).

3. If your score is 9 or 10, your work is done. Otherwise, explore what elements of the planning fallacy (see below) you are currently subject to. Is it:

   • Wishful thinking about scope?
   • Overconfidence in team abilities?
   • Social pressure (from leadership or team members)?
   • Avoidance ("if I take a close look, it's going to be ugly")?

4. What is the one thing your team can do to increase the accuracy of your timelines and estimates by ten percent? Agree on a simple next step.

5. Check in on your progress at your next meeting.

Background

First defined by Daniel Kahneman and Amos Tversky in 1979,[60] the planning fallacy says that humans routinely underestimate the amount of time needed to get a task done.

The planning fallacy is a wicked combination of wishful thinking, overconfidence, and convenience. The dynamics of organizational life don't help much, since executives are eager to get a rosy picture of the future and teams are eager to provide one.

By routinely breaking the work down into smaller pieces, methodologies like Agile and Lean reduce the impact of the planning fallacy. But the human psyche doesn't give up easily on its desire to overlook the truth in favor of skipping down the primrose path.

Cognitive bias is a given of our experience, and the planning fallacy is no more susceptible to easy or rapid elimination than any other form of bias. While the micropractice above will shift things in the near term, the longer-term remedy takes commitment and perseverance:

- Cultivate self-awareness, humility, and honesty so your team can recognize the planning fallacy when it shows up. Acknowledge that projects very often take longer than you think they will or want them to.
- Cultivate psychological safety on your team and beyond, so you can name planning bias when you see it, no matter how inconvenient that may be. (See page 196 for more about psychological safety.)
- Stay committed to seeking out and acting on the truth as the project proceeds, recognizing that you'll be forever swimming against the tide of fallacious thinking.

The planning fallacy is a tough nut to crack, but you can only gain by applying your attention to address it. To the extent that you can offset its effects, your team will likely deliver faster and more valuable results by avoiding scheduling problems, errors, and rework. But even if that success is limited, exercising the skills of self-awareness, critical thinking, and honesty will make your team stronger and more resilient.

Pay Attention to Honesty and Humility

Ask yourself hard questions about what you know and how you know it.

The Practice

Consider a decision you made recently that proved to be incorrect, or an assumption that turned out to be false. In a spirit of inquiry and to gain clarity for the future, take 10 minutes to write your answers to the following questions. You might do this as preparation for a retrospective. You also might ask some of the people you work with to answer the same questions about you. That will give you even more insight!

1. What might you have done to show more respect for the truth?
    *   Would gathering more data have made you more honest?
    *   Would another conversation (or several) have made you more honest?
    *   How could you have examined your assumptions more carefully?
    *   What pressures or challenges were you facing that made respect for the truth difficult?
2. What might you have done to think and act with more humility?
    *   What did you assume you knew, when in fact you didn't (or maybe couldn't) know?

- How could you have dialed back your certainty and conviction as you approached the situation?
- Were there times you were talking when you should have been listening?

Background

The cognitive biases we carry with us are certainly inconvenient. They call into question one of the aspects of our experience we are generally most proud of: the quality of our thinking. Our thought-stream has contributed so much to our evolutionary success that it's not surprising that we place it in high esteem. But the result of this confidence is that terms like "honesty" and "humility" are rarely trending on Google.

And yet these old-fashioned words are powerful antidotes to cognitive bias. They are perfectly suited to help us develop the habit of pausing and noticing, "What am I actually thinking and saying right now? What do I actually know?"

Let's define honesty as "respect for the truth." Part of that respect is recognizing that everyone brings bias to their judgments and decisions. Claims of honesty are delusional at best when they don't acknowledge the built-in human tendency to skew the truth for individual purposes. Genuine honesty means you seek out the truth as carefully and thoroughly as you can, doing your best to avoid jumping to conclusions.

Humility—the knowledge that, no matter how good your intentions, you will miss important things—is the logical companion of honesty: "knowing that you don't know." In combination, the two amount to an attitude that says: "I intend to find out and speak from the truth of this situation—and I'm fully aware that, despite my intention, there are gaps in my understanding."

Pay Attention to Your Team's Wisdom

Create a level playing field in meetings by engaging in deliberative thinking.

The Practice

The next time your team has a difficult conversation (a challenging retrospective, or a tough decision to make, or an internal conflict to address), allocate 30-60 minutes to a session where you use these wisdom council principles. Write them on the whiteboard. Hold yourselves accountable to abide by them.

1. **Speak from the heart.** Take the time to reflect on what is really true for you, as a whole person, and allow yourself to see what you have to say before you say it.

2. **Speak to the heart.** Recognize you are speaking not just to abstract representations of various points of view, but actual people who bring their own complex constellations of thought and experience to the discussion.

3. **Focus on the responsibility of this group, right here, right now.** Don't get caught up in what happened yesterday, what might happen tomorrow, or whose fault it is.

4. **Recognize the presence of power relationships.** If you hold organizational power, be cautious about using it when you are in council; if you don't have power, see if you can find the courage to speak up boldly, within reason. The goal is to create a balance among the voices in the group.

5. **Honor the principle of equal time.** One way to equalize power is to give all speakers an equal opportunity to speak. Use a stopwatch if you need to.

6. **Carry forward the council principles in your follow-up.** If you have unlimited time, continue the council as long as necessary. Since unlimited time is often not an option, make an agreement to continue the spirit of council as you take your next steps (whether that's decision-making, or planning, or action).

Background

Daniel Kahneman's book *Thinking Fast and Slow*[61] presents a compelling, deeply researched argument that human brains have two systems for engaging in thinking. What he calls "System 1" is fast, instinctive and emotional. "System 2" is slower, more deliberative, and more logical. System 1 is the source of a lot of our cognitive bias—the shortcuts we use to make quick decisions—as well as the emotional reactivity that leads us to act and speak without deliberation.

Deliberative thinking can be hard to come by when you're working on a high-pressure initiative. Usually "thinking fast" is more highly valued. What would it mean for your team to make the choice to slow down periodically so you can access system 2 thinking?

One method is the practice of a "wisdom council" protocol. Indigenous and traditional cultures around the world have made use of this set of tools for millennia, in which groups engage in deep reflection and create space for thoughtful discourse and dialogue. Sometimes thinking fast is a necessity, but the council tradition can teach us a lot about thinking slow.

SELF-AWARENESS

 Pay Attention to Body Sensations

Learn to notice the information coming to your brain from inside your body.

The Practice

1. Set aside two minutes when you can be undisturbed in a comfortable place.
2. Close your eyes.
3. Starting at your head, slowly scan your body from head to foot.
4. Pay special attention to any feelings of discomfort: tension, nausea, pain, dizziness—anything that seems a bit confused or turbulent.
5. You don't need to draw any conclusions from what you're noticing. Just investigate the sensations in detail and with curiosity.

Background

The first time I walked into a pachinko parlor—a form of pinball popular in Japan—the experience was almost overwhelming. Colored lights were flashing everywhere. There was an incredible roar of bells and buzzers and music and the rattle of thousands of little steel balls. After I'd been there for a while, though, some structure began to emerge. I started to notice the players, hunched over and mesmerized. I could pick out the electronic

J-Pop melodies and bells coming from the different machines. I wouldn't say I ever felt quite comfortable, but the whole scene did seem a lot more coherent.

At first, tuning in to the subtle signals your body sends your brain might be as hard to decipher as the cacophony that greets you when you walk into a pachinko parlor. There are random twinges and floods of energy, sinking and rising feelings, swirls and pirouettes of nausea and giddiness.

But, if you keep paying attention, some order starts to emerge. It's important to hang in there with the initial confusion. Otherwise you'll just turn and run back to the comfort of your routine thought-stream, stay disconnected from your body, and miss some potentially important signals.

Take note of any sensations coming to you from your body. Your brain responds to those sensations by turning them into emotional meanings and those meanings can drive you to take action. The decision to act in anger, or run for cover, starts with a sensation in your body. Noticing the original sensation sooner gives you more of a chance to view both the sensation and the impulse to respond with clarity, so you can make a conscious choice as to what to do about them.

Even if you make your living with your head, you can't afford to disregard your body. Particularly if you're involved in complex collaborative work, you need to stay in touch with the physical sensations you experience—the dryness in your mouth, the tightness in your throat, or the lump in your stomach. These are important clues to how your emotions are affecting your clarity of thought, your decisions, and your relationships. With this information you can take action to manage whatever obstacles are getting in your way.

Getting better at paying attention to body experiences is a valuable aspect of various kinds of mindfulness and other attention-building practices. A full head-to-toe body scan is one common practice. But when you're at work and fully engaged in thinking, it can be a little challenging to do this. You can always step out of the office, down the hall, out on the street. But the closer you can bring your body awareness to the work you actually do, the more effective it will be.

One strategy is to get accustomed to doing a simple quick check-in that emerges naturally from what you do day to day. If you're in a daily standup meeting, use that time to really feel your feet. If you spend a lot of time at your desk, take a few moments a couple of times a day to notice the familiar sensations of sitting so they become a little less familiar and a little more interesting. If you do a lot of typing, move your shoulders to bring awareness away from your fingers (they operate much like mini-brains, always in motion, always fiddling) and closer to your core. Even a little awareness in any part of your body makes it more possible to notice what else is going on—such as the sensations that accompany fear, anger, or resistance.

Pay Attention to What Triggers You

Uncover the ways your personal history shapes your reactions.

The Practice

1. As you go about your business one day, be on the lookout for little things other people do that cause a reaction in you that you recognize to be disproportionate. This might include:
    - Public behavior (for example, bad driving or aggressive cart-pushing in the grocery store).
    - Workplace behavior (for example, the loud talker or the messy-desk-keeper).
    - Specific behavior on your team (for example, email writing style, conference call habits).

2. Choose one specific item from the above that causes a reaction you want to explore further. Settle on an item that is:
    - Clear, concrete, and specific.
    - Almost guaranteed to cause a reaction in you.
    - Objectively harmless enough to make your reaction obviously excessive (even to you).

3. Write your answers to these questions:
    - What's the behavior you react to?
    - How do you react when you see it? What happens in your body? What thoughts come into your mind?
    - What incidents from the past might be adding fuel to your present reaction to this behavior? Be as specific as you can. Let yourself make creative associations. Also let yourself be unreasonably judgmental and petty—the way your brain stores memory is not necessarily rational!

4. The next time you observe the behavior, notice how your
    reaction has changed.

5. How might you apply this method to an interpersonal
    challenge with someone on your team?

Background

Your emotions are made of two things: the sensations in your
body, and the story you're telling yourself about those sensations.
And where does your story come from? Your memories. If you
were chased by an angry raccoon when you were young, you
probably have an iffy relationship with raccoons now.

Consider the places on the path of your life where you
encountered danger, difficulty, or exaltation. When you come to
new places that remind you of those, you're much more
susceptible to repeat experiences: a sort of déjà vu.

Being aware of the accumulated memories that stir up reactions
puts some space between you and the reactive emotions the new
circumstances evoke. It's not that the reaction won't occur, but
you can step back, see what's happening, and make a choice
about how to proceed.

There's no need to be comprehensive (that would be exhausting).
Just select a few memories or patterns to get more conscious
about, and investigate the effect those memories have on your
current experience. You'll become more aware, and that
awareness will help you moderate your reaction.

Pay Attention to Team Emotions

Acknowledge emotions—especially reactive emotions—in meetings in a safe and structured way.

The Practice

When difficult circumstances arise, propose adding a practice to address the presence of reactive emotions—fighting, fleeing, or freezing—to your team's agenda. Such circumstances might include:

- Conflict within the team, or with another team.
- Initiatives causing significant change to the group.
- Mergers, acquisitions, reorgs, or other organizational changes.
- Significant personnel changes on the team or in leadership.
- Significant pressure to deliver, or delivery problems.

Be sure to explain the process below clearly so everyone knows what's being proposed.

1. At the beginning of the meeting, name the issue that is the source of reactive emotion.
2. Set the context: "Since we're facing a situation that naturally stirs up reactive emotions, we're each going to name those reactions, and listen to each other attentively and without judgments."
3. Have each person in the room describe themselves with one of four statuses with regard to the issue:

- I'm fighting
- I'm fleeing
- I'm freezing
- I'm OK

4. Set the context: "Now we're going to have one volunteer go into a little more depth. The rest of us will listen attentively and without judgments."

5. Have one volunteer answer the questions below (excluding anyone who reports "I'm OK"):

   - What is causing your reaction?
   - Where do you notice the sensation in your body?
   - What help can we as a group give you to minimize any negative impacts?
   - What action can we as a group take to address the underlying cause?
   - What's helpful about noticing this?

6. Thank the volunteer and proceed with your normal meeting agenda.

7. In each meeting, have a different person volunteer. If it's helpful, you might establish a regular rotation.

Background

The term "emotional intelligence," popularized by Daniel Goleman in his 1996 book of the same name,[62] has come into common use in organizational life. It is a good thing emotions are becoming more widely recognized as part of human experience— even at work.

But, as often happens with popular concepts, the precision of some definitions has suffered somewhat through wide use. Here are some realities about emotional intelligence that will help you use its principles more effectively to build aligned teams.

First, the way emotions are expressed is highly variable across individuals as well as groups. "Intelligence" may suggest a single ranked scale of ability. As a combination of bodily sensation, memory, values, culture and much more, emotional expression is a particularly rich resource for accessing diverse points of view and experiences of life.

Second, emotions are a positive good in many situations, rather than being somehow inferior to cognitive activity, or merely an annoyance to be managed. Just the simple act of regarding emotions as important dimensions of team life, rather than a necessary evil to be endured, opens up many more possibilities. Emotional responses do take time to process, and they are often not initially or primarily verbal. But teams who attempt to suppress, discount or reason past the unique perspectives and points of view that emotions provide, run the risk of missing valuable insights.

Third, the capacity to work effectively with emotions can be developed by any individual. "Intelligence" implies an inborn ability (though we now know cognitive intelligence is much more fluid in adulthood than was once thought). The capacity to have awareness of emotions, find effective ways of articulating them, and put them to use to solve problems and generate insight is something any individual can develop. This is in fact what makes team life so interesting: a group of individuals, each with his or her own emotional capacity (developed as a result of genetics, upbringing, and other environmental factors), coming together to grow that capacity further in collaboration with others.

Pay Attention to Psychological Safety

Create a repeatable formula for monitoring and improving your team's psychological safety.

The Practice

Work with your team to create a psychological safety charter. Regularly review it and hold yourselves accountable to it. When new people join the team, orient them to the charter, and use that occasion to renew your commitment to it and make updates. Evaluate your progress.

A charter might look something like this:

> We intend to be a psychologically safe team, so individuals can take the personal risks we need them to take. We can't control all the circumstances that will make us feel safe or unsafe. Our goal is to create as much safety as we can in those circumstances, for everyone on this team and everyone we work with.

> In order to achieve this goal, we all commit to:

> - **Building our self-knowledge.** We will pay attention to the effect we have on others, and regularly check in if we aren't sure. We will also pay attention to our own experience of safety and take positive action to address that if we're not feeling safe.
> - **Listening to each other.** We will really hear and take in what other people are communicating: not just the words

they are using, but tone of voice, body language, and ary other emotional clues.

- **Including each other.** We will keep barriers down, stay transparent, and engage in rich interactions with one another to stimulate the growth of connection.
- **Speaking up for ourselves.** Each one of us takes responsibility for articulating our own point of view — especially when it's challenging to express in the moment—since each point of view is essential for making this team the best it can be.

Background

A compelling piece of recent research about team effectiveness comes from Google's Aristotle Project.[63] It's among the best and most thorough investigations of what makes corporate teams work well together. The key finding was that the number one predictor of team effectiveness is "psychological safety": the shared belief that the team is safe for interpersonal risk taking. There are other team effectiveness factors, too, like dependability and structure and clarity—but psychological safety tops the list. If we ever needed a reminder that humans today continue to live out the challenges of our ancestral, risk-filled homelands, this should do it. When people feel safe with each other, they perform well. When they don't, they can't.

While managers in particular have a definite impact on the sense of safety in a group, every member of the team has a role to play. Without a group exploration of safety or its absence, it's easy to view the lack of safety as someone else's problem. When everyone on a team takes responsibility for building a safe environment, teams can make real progress.

While the norms of safety may vary from one environment to another, a team's sense of psychological safety functions as a reservoir of goodwill and trust. Everyone on the team is always draining the reservoir, or they are filling it up.

NOTES

1 reWork: with Google, "re:Work - Guide: Understand team
   effectiveness," *re:Work:*, https://rework.withgoogle.com/guides/
   understanding-team-effectiveness/steps/identify-dynamics-of-effective-
   teams/

2 Irma Kornilova, "DevOps is a Culture, Not a Role!" *Medium*, April 28.
   2017, https://medium.com/@neonrocket/devops-is-a-culture-not-a-role-
   be1bed149b0; Frederico Toledo, "Why So Much Talk Around DevOps
   Culture?" *Dzone*, October 25, 2017, https://dzone.com/articles/why-so-
   much-talk-around-devops-culture

3 Juhani Iivari and Netta Iivari, "The Relationship Between
   Organizational Culture and the Deployment of Agile Methods,"
   Information and Software Technology 53 (2011) 509–520,
   http://robertfeld.net/courses/agile/Iivari_2011_ist.pdf; Nan Hatch, "10
   Critical Culture Change Elements in Agile Transformation," *Cardinal*,
   June 10, 2016, https://www.cardinalsolutions.com/blog/2016/06/10-
   critical-culture-change-elements-in-agile-transformation

4 Fahed Al-Duwailah and Maged Ali, "The Effect of Organizational
   Culture on CRM Success," *European, Mediterranean & Middle Eastern
   Conference on Information Systems 2013*,
   https://bura.brurel.ac.uk/bitstream/2438/8185/2/Fulltext.pdf

5 Jim Hemerling, Julie Kilmann, Martin Danoesastro, Liza Stutts, and
   Cailin Ahern, "It's Not a Digital Transformation Without a Digital
   Culture," Boston Consulting Group, April 13, 2018,
   https://www.bcg.com/en-us/publications/2018/not-digital-
   transformation-without-digital-culture.aspx

6 Shane Hastie and Stéphane Wojewoda, "Standish Group 2015 Chaos
   Report – Q&A with Jennifer Lynch," *InfoQ*, October 4, 2015,
   https://www.infoq.com/articles/standish-chaos-2015

7   Laurence Bradford, "Why We Need to Talk About Burnout in the Tech Industry," *Forbes*, June 19, 2018, https://www.forbes.com/sites/laurencebradford/2018/06/19/why-we-need-to-talk-about-burnout-in-the-tech-industry/

8   "Non-judgmental awareness" and "taking action" are not as contradictory as they might sound. We'll explore this further in the discussion of cognitive bias in Chapter Three.

9   The core definition of paying attention in chapter 1 as based on "present-moment, non-judgmental awareness" comes from Jon Kabat-Zinn's work. See his book *Mindfulness for Beginners* (Boulder, CO: Sounds True, 2016). See also Sharon Salzberg's *Real Happiness* (New York: Workman Pub., 2010).

10 Niklas Göke, "Why Trampelpfad Is the One German Word You Should Remember (For Boosting Your Willpower)," *Better Humans*, November 23, 2015, https://betterhumans.coach.me/why-trampelpfad-is-the-one-german-word-you-should-remember-for-boosting-your-willpower-c8afcd030b6f

11 Peter M. Milner, "The Discovery of Self-stimulation and Other Stories," *Neuroscience & Biobehavioral Reviews* 13, no. 2–3 (Summer 1989): 61–67, doi:10.1016/S0149-7634(89)80013-2

12 Andrew Thompson, "Engineers of Addiction," *The Verge*, https://www.theverge.com/2015/5/6/8544303/casino-slot-machine-gambling-addiction-psychology-mobile-games (accessed October 16, 2018).

13 See Jeremy Dean's book *Making Habits, Breaking Habits - How to Make Changes That Stick* (Boston: Da Capo, 2013). See also Maria Popova, "How Long It Takes to Form a New Habit," *Brain Pickings*, https://www.brainpickings.org/2014/01/02/how-long-it-takes-to-form-a-new-habit/ (accessed November 11, 2018).

14 See Daniel Goleman's book Focus: The Hidden Power of Excellence (Bloomsbury, 2014) for an extensive exploration.

15 Marcus E. Raichle et al., "A Default Mode of Brain Function," *Proceedings of the National Academy of Sciences*, Jan 2001, 98 (2) 676-682. See also Virginia Hughes, "The Brain's Dark Energy," *National Geographic*, October 6, 2010, https://www.nationalgeographic.com/science/phenomena/2010/10/06/brain-default-mode/

16 Adele Diamond, "Executive Functions," *Annual Review of Psychology* 64: 135–168, doi:10.1146/anr.urev-psych-113011-143750

17 Plato, Phaedrus 246a–254e, in Plato in Twelve Volumes, Vol. 9, trans Harold N. Fowler (Cambridge, MA, Harvard University Press. 1925).

18 See John Medina's *Brain Rules: 12 Principles for Surviving and Thriving at Work, Home, and School* (Seattle: Pear Press, 2014), pp. 17-36, for more on this topic.

19 The material in this section is based in part on the e-book *Mindful Habits for 7 Lean Practices*, which I co-authored with Todd Hudson of the Maverick Institute. It's available via my website, www.jhanderson.biz.

20 United Nations Office on Drugs and Crime, *Global Study on Homicide 2013*, https://www.unodc.org/documents/gsh/pdfs/2014_GLOBAL_HOMICIDE_BOOK_web.pdf

21 David Gendelman, "Why Does Every Soccer Player Do This?" *New York Times*, July 10, 2018, https://www.nytimes.com/2018/07/10/sports/world-cup/england-croatia-france-belgium.html

22 One among many layers of this complexity is suggested by Zonglei Zhen, Huizher Fang, and Jia Liu, "The Hierarchical Brain Network for Face Recognition," *PLOS | One*, March 20, 2013, doi:10.1371/journal.pone.0059886

23 All of this from psychologist David Perrett's TED talk, https://www.youtube.com/watch?v=rVE6kZW88lc

24 "Eying Up the Collaboration," *The Economist*, November 2, 2006, https://www.economist.com/science-and-technology/2006/11/02/eyeing-up-the-collaboration

25 Carsten K. W. De Dreu, et al, "Oxytocin Promotes Human Ethnocentrism," *Proceedings of the National Academy of Sciences*, January 25, 2011, doi:10.1073/pnas.1015316108; Shaul Shalvi and Carsten K. W. De Dreu, "Oxytocin Promotes Group-Serving Dishonesty," *Proceedings of the National Academy of Sciences*, April 15, 2014, doi:10.1073/pnas.1400724111

26 "A Conversation with Naomi Eisenberger," *Edge*, September 10, 2014, https://www.edge.org/conversation/naomi_eisenberger-social-pain; Emily Esfahani Smith, "Social Connection Makes a Better Brain," *The Atlantic*, October 29, 2013, https://www.theatlantic.com/health/archive/2013/10/social-connection-makes-a-better-brain/280934/

27 A nice summary of theory of mind, focused on Band-aids, pigs, and 3-year-olds, is Brittany M. Thompson's "Theory of Mind: Understanding Others in a Social World," *Psychology Today*, July 3, 2017, https://www.psychologytoday.com/us/blog/socioemotionalsuccess/201707/theory-mind-understanding-others-in-social-world

28 See http://agilemanifesto.org/.

29 See https://www.scrum.org/.

30 Lisa Feldman Barrett, *How Emotions Are Made: The Secret Life of the Brain* (Boston: Houghton Mifflin Harcourt, 2016), Chapter 4, "The Origin of Feeling."

31 Anil Seth, "Your Brain Hallucinates Your Conscious Reality," TED, April 2017, https://www.ted.com/talks/anil_seth_how_your_brain_hallucinates_your_conscious_reality

32 Barrett, How Emotions Are Made: The Secret Life of the Brain, Chapter 4, "The Origin of Feeling."

33 Tara Parker-Pope, "What Clown on a Unicycle? Studying Cellphone Distraction," *New York Times*, October 22, 2009, https://well.blogs.nytimes.com/2009/10/22/what-clown-on-a-unicycle-studying-cell-phone-distraction/ (This article points out that only 8% of cell phone users noticed the clown. But that's a different story.)

34 Image © 1995, Edward H. Adelson. See http://persci.mit.edu/gallery/checkershadow

35 "List of Cognitive Biases," Wikipedia, https://en.wikipedia.org/wiki/List_of_cognitive_biases (accessed July 11, 2018). For a somewhat shorter but no less daunting list, see Eric Fernandez, "Cognitive Biases: A Visual Study Guide," *Scribd*, "https://www.scribd.com/doc/30548590/Cognitive-Biases-A-Visual-Study-Guide (accessed December 11, 2018).

36 Here's a good recent article: Ben Yagoda, "The Cognitive Biases Tricking Your Brain," *The Atlantic*, September 2018, https://www.theatlantic.com/magazine/archive/2018/09/cognitive-bias/565775/

37 This theory was developed by Robert Trivers. See "TEDxJamaica - Robert Trivers -Deceit and Self-deception: Fooling Ourselves the Better to Fool Others," YouTube, December 10, 2010, https://www.youtube.com/watch?v=dAljJfR3HZ0

38 "Understanding Implicit Bias," Kirwan Institute for the Study of Race and Ethnicity, http://kirwaninstitute.osu.edu/research/understanding-implicit-bias/ (accessed October 11, 2018).

39 Celeste Kidd and Benjamin Y. Hayden, "The Psychology and Neuroscience of Curiosity," *Neuron*, 2015 Nov 4; 88(3): 449–460, doi:10.1016/j.neuron.2015.09.010

40 Personal communication. See www.theyesworks.com. For more about dopamine see page 17.

41 For much more on the mischievous nature of the amygdala and its ability to remember, see Robert Sapolsky, *Behave: The Biology of Humans at Our Best and Worst* (London: Vintage, 2018), chapter 2, "One Second Before."

42 Barrett, *How Emotions Are Made*, chapter 5, "Concepts, Goals, and Words."

43 Body outline designed by Freepik, https://www.freepik.com/free-vector/silhouettes-of-man-and-woman_766045.htm

44 This example comes from the Center for Nonviolent Communication's "Feelings Inventory." See https://www.cnvc.org/Training/feelings-inventory for the full list.

45   Ben Mulholland, "8 Critical Change Management Models to Evolve and Survive," Process.St, July 24, 2017, https://www.process.st/change-management-models/ The summary that follows in the text is based on this excellent article, which has links to further resources on each model.

46   Dale Stafford and Laura Miles, "Integrating Cultures After a Merger," Bain & Company, December 11, 2013, https://www.bain.com/insights/integrating-cultures-after-a-merger/

47   See Timothy J. Galpin and Mark Herndon, *The Complete Guide to Mergers and Acquisitions: Process Tools to Support M&A Integration at Every Level* (San Francisco: Jossey Bass, 2007) and Ted Rouse and Tory Frame, "The 10 Steps to Successful M&A Integration," Bain & Company, November 4, 2009, https://www.bain.com/insights/10-steps-to-successful-ma-integration/

48   "Loss aversion" is the psychological theory that people prefer avoiding loss to acquiring equivalent gains. See Daniel Kahneman and Amos Tversky, "Prospect Theory: An Analysis of Decision under Risk," *Econometrica*, 47 (4): 263–291. doi:10.2307/1914185 This idea has been further developed by Marty Linsky, through the concept of "leadership as the distribution of loss." See Marty Linsky, "Leadership as the Distribution of Loss," Linsky on Leadership, September 7, 2009, http://cambridgeleadership.blogspot.com/2009/09/leadership-as-distribution-of-loss.html

49   Angeles Arrien, The Four-Fold Way: Walking the Paths of the Warrior, Teacher, Healer, and Visionary, (HarperSanFrancisco, 1993), Chapter 2, "The Way of the Healer."

50   Joseph H. Anderson, *The Mindful Office*, 2017. Available at http://jhanderson.biz/index.php/the-mindful-office/

51   Jennifer Sprecher of the University of Washington recently shared with me that she encourages people to keep their phones and laptops out and open during meetings. "It's a great way to determine whether the meeting is truly engaging or not. When someone's attention drops away, we all know we have to do a better job."

52   Leslie A. Perlow, Constance Noonan Hadley, and Eunice Eun, "Stop the Meeting Madness," *Harvard Business Review*, https://hbr.org/2017/07/stop-the-meeting-madness (accessed November 7, 2018).

53 This practice is adapted from Salzberg, *Real Happiness*.

54 Shannon Vallor, *Technology and the Virtues: A Philosophical Guide to a Future Worth Wanting*, (New York: Oxford University Press, 2016), chapter 6, "Technomoral Wisdom for an Uncertain Future: 21st Century Virtues."

55 Rick Hanson, *Hardwiring Happiness* (New York: Random House USA, 2015), chapter 4, "HEAL Yourself."

56 See the website https://sirenofshame.com/Products. You can buy "The Big Siren," "The Small Siren," or "The Mug."

57 Leo Cassarini, "Indicate your build status with programmable light bulbs," *Geckoboard*, January 20, 2014, https://www.geckoboard.com/blog/indicate-your-build-status-with-programmable-light-bulbs/

58 Hanson, *Hardwiring Happiness*, chapter 1, "Growing Good."

59 "The Power of Positivity, In Moderation: The Losada Ratio," *Happier Human*, http://happierhuman.com/losada-ratio/ (accessed December 14, 2018).

60 Daniel Kahneman and Amos Tversky, "Intuitive prediction: biases and corrective procedures," *TIMS Studies in Management Science*, 12: 313–327. See also Mark V. Pezzo, Jordan A. Litman, and Stephanie P. Pezzo, "On the Distinction Between Yuppies and Hippies: Individual Differences in Prediction Biases for Planning Future Tasks," *Personality and Individual Differences*, 41 (7): 1359–1371, doi:10.1016/j.paid.2006.03.029

61 Daniel Kahneman, *Thinking, Fast and Slow* (New York: Farrar, Straus and Giroux, 2011).

62 Daniel Goleman, *Emotional Intelligence* (New York: Bantam Books, 1995).

63 reWork: with Google, "re:Work - Guide: Understand team effectiveness."

FURTHER READING

BOOKS

Anderson, Joseph H. *The Mindful Office* (Seattle, 2017).

Anderson, Joseph H., and Todd Hudson. *Mindful Habits for 7 Lean Practices.* (Seattle, 2018).

Arrien, Angeles. *The Four-Fold Way: Walking the Paths of the Warrior, Teacher, Healer, and Visionary.* (HarperSanFrancisco, 1993).

Barrett, Lisa Feldman. *How Emotions Are Made: The Secret Life of the Brain* (Boston: Houghton Mifflin Harcourt, 2016).

Dean, Jeremy. *Making Habits, Breaking Habits - How to Make Changes That Stick* (Boston: Da Capo, 2013).

Goleman Daniel. *Emotional Intelligence* (New York: Bantam Books, 1995).

————. *Focus: The Hidden Power of Excellence* (Bloomsbury, 2014).

Hanson, Rick. *Hardwiring Happiness* (New York: Random House USA, 2015).

Kabat-Zinn, Jon. *Mindfulness for Beginners* (Boulder, CO: Sounds True, 2016).

Kahneman, Daniel *Thinking, Fast and Slow* (New York: Farrar, Straus and Giroux, 2011).

Medina, John. *Brain Rules: 12 Principles for Surviving and Thriving at Work, Home, and School* (Seattle: Pear Press, 2014).

Salzberg, Sharon. *Real Happiness* (New York: Workman Pub., 2010).

Sapolsky, Robert. *Behave: The Biology of Humans at Our Best and Worst* (London: Vintage, 2018).

Vallor, Shannon. *Technology and the Virtues: A Philosophical Guide to a Future Worth Wanting* (New York: Oxford University Press, 2016).

ARTICLES

"A Conversation with Naomi Eisenberger." *Edge,* September 10, 2014. https://www.edge.org/conversation/naomi_eisenberger-social-pain

"List of Cognitive Biases." Wikipedia. https://en.wikipedia.org/wiki/List_of_cognitive_biases (accessed July 11, 2018).

"The Power of Positivity, In Moderation: The Losada Ratio." *Happier Human.* http://happierhuman.com/losada-ratio/ (accessed December 14, 2018).

"Understanding Implicit Bias." Kirwan Institute for the Study of Race and Ethnicity. http://kirwaninstitute.osu.edu/research/understanding-implicit-bias/ (accessed October 11, 2018).

Center for Nonviolent Communication. "Feelings Inventory." https://www.cnvc org/Training/feelings-inventory

De Dreu, Carsten K. W., et al. "Oxytocin Promotes Human Ethnocentrism." *Proceedings of the National Academy of Sciences,* January 25, 2011. doi:10.1073/pnas.1015316108

Diamond, Adele. "Executive Functions." *Annual Review of Psychology* 64: 135–168. doi:10.1146/annurev-psych-113011-143750

Esfahani Smith, Emily. "Social Connection Makes a Better Brain." *The Atlantic*, October 29, 2013. https://www.theatlantic.com/health/archive/2013/10/social-connection-makes-a-better-brain/280934/

Fernandez, Eric. "Cognitive Biases: A Visual Study Guide." *Scribd*. "https://www.scribd.com/doc/30548590/Cognitive-Biases-A-Visual-Study-Guide (accessed December 11, 2018).

Gendelman, David. "Why Does Every Soccer Player Do This?" *New York Times*, July 10, 2018. https://www.nytimes.com/2018/07/10/sports/world-cup/england-croatia-france-belgium.html

Hughes, Virginia. "The Brain's Dark Energy." *National Geographic*, October 6, 2010. https://www.nationalgeographic.com/science/phenomena/2010/10/06/brain-default-mode/

Kahneman, Daniel, and Amos Tversky. "Intuitive prediction: biases and corrective procedures." *TIMS Studies in Management Science*, 12: 313–327.

———. "Prospect Theory: An Analysis of Decision under Risk." *Econometrica*, 47 (4): 263–291. doi:10.2307/1914185

Kidd, Celeste, and Benjamin Y. Hayden. "The Psychology and Neuroscience of Curiosity." *Neuron*, 2015 Nov 4; 88(3): 449–460. doi:10.1016/j.neuron.2015.09.010

Linsky, Marty. "Leadership as the Distribution of Loss." Linsky on Leadership, September 7, 2009. http://cambridgeleadership.blogspot.com/2009/09/leadership-as-distribution-of-loss.html

Milner, Peter M. "The Discovery of Self-stimulation and Other Stories." *Neuroscience & Biobehavioral Reviews* 13, no. 2–3 (Summer 1989): 61–67. doi:10.1016/S0149-7634(89)80013-2

Mulholland, Ben. "8 Critical Change Management Models to Evolve and Survive." Process.St, July 24, 2017. https://www.process.st/change-management-models/

Parker-Pope, Tara. "What Clown on a Unicycle? Studying Cellphone Distraction." *New York Times*, October 22, 2009. https://well.blogs.

nytimes.com/2009/10/22/what-clown-on-a-unicycle-studying-cell-phone-distraction/

Pezzo, Mark V., Jordan A. Litman, and Stephanie P. Pezzo. "On the Distinction Between Yuppies and Hippies: Individual Differences in Prediction Biases for Planning Future Tasks." *Personality and Individual Differences*, 41 (7): 1359–1371. doi:10.1016/j.paid.2006.03.029

Popova, Maria. "How Long It Takes to Form a New Habit." *Brain Pickings*. https://www.brainpickings.org/2014/01/02/how-long-it-takes-to-form-a-new-habit/ (accessed November 11, 2018).

Raichle, Marcus E., et al. "A Default Mode of Brain Function." *Proceedings of the National Academy of Sciences*, Jan 2001, 98 (2) 676-682.

Seth, Anil. "Your Brain Hallucinates Your Conscious Reality." TED, April 2017. https://www.ted.com/talks/anil_seth_how_your_brain_hallucinates_your_conscious_reality

Shalvi, Shaul, and Carsten K. W. De Dreu. "Oxytocin Promotes Group-Serving Dishonesty." *Proceedings of the National Academy of Sciences*, April 15, 2014. doi:10.1073/pnas.1400724111

Thompson, Andrew. "Engineers of Addiction." *The Verge*, https://www.theverge.com/2015/5/6/8544303/casino-slot-machine-gambling-addiction-psychology-mobile-games (accessed October 16, 2018).

Thompson, Brittany M. "Theory of Mind: Understanding Others in a Social World." *Psychology Today*, July 3, 2017. https://www.psychologytoday.com/us/blog/socioemotional-success/201707/theory-mind-understanding-others-in-social-world

Yagoda, Ben. "The Cognitive Biases Tricking Your Brain." *The Atlantic*, September 2018. https://www.theatlantic.com/magazine/archive/2018/09/cognitive-bias/565775/

Zhen, Zonglei, Huizhen Fang, and Jia Liu. "The Hierarchical Brain Network for Face Recognition." *PLOS | One*, March 20, 2013. doi:10.1371/journal.pone.0059886

ACKNOWLEDGEMENTS

I'm grateful to the remarkable people who contributed their good ideas to this book, provided wonderful feedback, and otherwise kept me going through the book-writing process. I couldn't have done it without the help of the people listed below, and many others too numerous to mention.

Todd Hudson generously invited me to co-write a book on mindfulness and Lean with him a year ago, and the experience of that project led directly to this one. It was Bryan Brewer and Chris Cancialosi telling me in no uncertain terms that I needed to write a book that sealed the deal.

Joel Grow of the Seattle Mindfulness Center, Sophie Leroy of the University of Washington's School of Business, and Michael Kelberer and Tim Burnett of Mindfulness Northwest provided valuable input on the connections between mindfulness and workplace effectiveness that were the seeds of this book. Cory Custer and Dan DiCamillo helped me think more deeply about those connections. Dan Leahy's teaching and mentorship around the principles of Adaptive Leadership are always lurking in the background of this book (though they never quite made it into the text). University of Washington neuroscientist John Medina gave me feedback and stimulated new thinking about the brain science concepts in this book.

My fellow members of SeattleCoach cohort 28, Peter Berry, Chris Cancialosi, Molly Huber, Peyina Lin-Roberts, Phoebe Sade-Anderson, Phyllis Turner-Brim, Jeanne Yu, along with our teachers Julie Stringham, Janet Williams-Hepler, and Patricia Burgin, gave me much wise counsel and support as the seeds were germinating.

ACKNOWLEDGEMENTS 211

The Seattle Lean Coffee and Seattle CoffeeOps meetups provided numerous conversations about real-world workplace challenges, as well as places of community on the solitary journey of writing. Don O'Neill and Bart Ozretich gave me encouragement at crucial moments on that journey, and Josh Gidding, Darren Varnado, and David Scott Bernstein generously gave me invaluable mentorship.

Dawn Kinsey, Nayaab Lokhandwala, Anna Marshall, Andrew Petersen, and Jennifer Sprecher helped me think more deeply about what paying attention means to teams and how to make changes stick.

Bob Boiko, Alexander Jones, Margaret Marcuson, Alan Marks, Linda Merrick, and Joel VanDerAa read my manuscript and gave me feedback that was instrumental in making the book much better than it would have been otherwise.

Waverly Fitzgerald provided an excellent editorial review.

Among the many satisfactions of writing this book has been the opportunity to reflect on the experiences I've had in the past few decades working with technology organizations. These experiences lie behind the tales told in the book, including Terra's story. I'm grateful to all the co-workers and leaders who have shown me, through examples good and bad, what makes teams work.

Victoria Scarlett designed the book's cover and contents, and provided much invaluable editorial help. By an extraordinary stroke of good fortune, she is not just an amazingly talented collaborator but also my best friend, life partner, and a source of continual inspiration. This book is dedicated to her.

ABOUT THE AUTHOR

Joseph H. Anderson is the author of *The Mindful Office* and (with Todd Hudson) the co-author of *Mindful Habits for 7 Lean Practices*. He has explored the cultivation of attention in the corporate workplace since he began his technology career in 1989. As a departmental manager, program manager, and consultant, he has helped teams in many organizations find greater harmony and effectiveness while leading them through complex enterprise technology integration, change management, and business development initiatives. Organizations he has worked with include Microsoft, the Bill & Melinda Gates Foundation, The Boeing Company, the University of Washington, and Getty Images.

In parallel with his work in the tech industry, Joe has spent more than a decade leading and teaching dozens of workshops in Gregorian chant, helping groups of singers (many of them new to singing) find their way to the profound experience of true unison by connecting with others through vocal sound.

Joe's current work is training and coaching technology and cross-functional teams to pay better attention as they work together. This work brings the practices of deep awareness he has cultivated as a master chant teacher into the diverse and pressure-laden world of the contemporary technology workplace.

Made in the USA
Middletown, DE
23 February 2019